MznLnx

Missing Links Exam Preps

Exam Prep for

Algebra

Artin, 1st Edition

The MznLnx Exam Prep is your link from the texbook and lecture to your exams.
The MznLnx Exam Preps are unauthorized and comprehensive reviews of your textbooks.

All material provided by MznLnx and Rico Publications (c) 2010
Textbook publishers and textbook authors do not particpate in or contribute to these reviews.

MznLnx

Rico
Publications

Exam Prep for Algebra
1st Edition
Artin

Publisher: Raymond Houge
Assistant Editor: Michael Rouger
Text and Cover Designer: Lisa Buckner
Marketing Manager: Sara Swagger
Project Manager, Editorial Production: Jerry Emerson
Art Director: Vernon Lowerui

Product Manager: Dave Mason
Editorial Assitant: Rachel Guzmanji
Pedagogy: Debra Long
Cover Image: Jim Reed/Getty Images
Text and Cover Printer: City Printing, Inc.
Compositor: Media Mix, Inc.

(c) 2010 Rico Publications
ALL RIGHTS RESERVED. No part of this work covered by the copyright may be reproduced or used in any form or by an means--graphic, electronic, or mechanical, including photocopying, recording, taping, Web distribution, information storage, and retrieval systems, or in any other manner--without the written permission of the publisher.

Printed in the United States
ISBN:

For more information about our products, contact us at:
Dave.Mason@RicoPublications.com

For permission to use material from this text or product, submit a request online to:
Dave.Mason@RicoPublications.com

Contents

CHAPTER 1
Matrix Operations 1
CHAPTER 2
Groups 10
CHAPTER 3
Vector Spaces 22
CHAPTER 4
Linear Transformations 32
CHAPTER 5
Symmetry 46
CHAPTER 6
More Group Theory 62
CHAPTER 7
Bilinear Forms 74
CHAPTER 8
Linear Groups 87
CHAPTER 9
Group Representations 103
CHAPTER 10
Rings 116
CHAPTER 11
Factorization 118
CHAPTER 12
Modules 120
CHAPTER 13
Fields 121
CHAPTER 14
Galois Theory 123
ANSWER KEY 125

TO THE STUDENT

COMPREHENSIVE

The *MznLnx* Exam Prep series is designed to help you pass your exams. Editors at MznLnx review your textbooks and then prepare these practice exams to help you master the textbook material. Unlike study guides, workbooks, and practice tests provided by the texbook publisher and textbook authors, *MznLnx* gives you **all** of the material in each chapter in exam form, not just samples, so you can be sure to nail your exam.

MECHANICAL

The MznLnx Exam Prep series creates exams that will help you learn the subject matter as well as test you on your understanding. Each question is designed to help you master the concept. Just working through the exams, you gain an understanding of the subject--its a simple mechanical process that produces success.

INTEGRATED STUDY GUIDE AND REVIEW

MznLnx is not just a set of exams designed to test you, its also a comprehensive review of the subject content. Each exam question is also a review of the concept, making sure that you will get the answer correct without having to go to other sources of material. You learn as you go! Its the easiest way to pass an exam.

HUMOR

Studying can be tedious and dry. MznLnx's instructional design includes moderate humor within the exam questions on occassion, to break the tedium and revitalize the brain

Chapter 1. Matrix Operations 1

1. In mathematics, _____ is an elementary arithmetic operation. When one of the numbers is a whole number, _____ is the repeated sum of the other number.
   - a. Thing
   - b. Multiplication0
   - c. Undefined
   - d. Undefined

2. In mathematics, a _____ is a rectangular table of numbers or, more generally, a table consisting of abstract quantities that can be added and multiplied.
   - a. Thing
   - b. Matrix0
   - c. Undefined
   - d. Undefined

3. In algebra, a _____ is a function depending on *n* that associates a scalar, det(A), to every *n×n* square matrix A.
   - a. Determinant0
   - b. Thing
   - c. Undefined
   - d. Undefined

4. In mathematics, a matrix can be thought of as each row or _____ being a vector. Hence, a space formed by row vectors or _____ vectors are said to be a row space or a _____ space.
   - a. Column0
   - b. Concept
   - c. Undefined
   - d. Undefined

5. In computer science an _____ is a data structure that consists of a group of elements having a single name that are accessed by indexing. In most programming languages each element has the same data type and the _____ occupies a continuous area of storage.
   - a. Array0
   - b. Thing
   - c. Undefined
   - d. Undefined

6. The _____ are the only integral domain whose positive elements are well-ordered, and in which order is preserved by addition. Like the natural numbers, the _____ form a countably infinite set. The set of all _____ is usually denoted in mathematics by a boldface Z .
   - a. Integers0
   - b. Thing
   - c. Undefined
   - d. Undefined

7. The word _____ is used in a variety of ways in mathematics.
   - a. Index0
   - b. Thing
   - c. Undefined
   - d. Undefined

8. In physics and in _____ calculus, a spatial _____, or simply _____, is a concept characterized by a magnitude and a direction.
   - a. Vector0
   - b. Thing
   - c. Undefined
   - d. Undefined

9. In linear algebra, real numbers are called scalars and relate to vectors in a vector space through the operation of _____ multiplication, in which a vector can be multiplied by a number to produce another vector.
   - a. Thing
   - b. Scalar0
   - c. Undefined
   - d. Undefined

10. _____ is one of the basic operations defining a vector space in linear algebra.

a. Scalar multiplication0
b. Thing
c. Undefined
d. Undefined

11. The _____ (symbol _____) and the millibar (symbol mbar, also mb) are units of pressure.
    a. Bar0
    b. Thing
    c. Undefined
    d. Undefined

12. A _____ is a function that assigns a number to subsets of a given set.
    a. Thing
    b. Measure0
    c. Undefined
    d. Undefined

13. In mathematics, a _____ is the result of multiplying, or an expression that identifies factors to be multiplied.
    a. Product0
    b. Thing
    c. Undefined
    d. Undefined

14. Mathematical _____ is used to represent ideas.
    a. Notation0
    b. Thing
    c. Undefined
    d. Undefined

15. The word _____ comes from the Latin word linearis, which means created by lines.
    a. Thing
    b. Linear0
    c. Undefined
    d. Undefined

16. A _____ is an equation in which each term is either a constant or the product of a constant times the first power of a variable.
    a. Thing
    b. Linear equation0
    c. Undefined
    d. Undefined

17. In mathematics, a subset of Euclidean space R^n is called _____ if it is closed and bounded.
    a. Thing
    b. Compact0
    c. Undefined
    d. Undefined

18. _____ is a property that a binary operation can have.
    a. Associative law0
    b. Thing
    c. Undefined
    d. Undefined

19. An _____ is an equality that remains true regardless of the values of any variables that appear within it, to distinguish it from an equality which is true under more particular conditions.
    a. Identity0
    b. Thing
    c. Undefined
    d. Undefined

20. The _____ relates to the binary operation of multiplication and addition.
    a. Thing
    b. Distributive law0
    c. Undefined
    d. Undefined

Chapter 1. Matrix Operations

21. The _____ is a rule which states that when you add or multiply numbers, changing the order doesn't change the result.
    a. Commutative law0
    b. Thing
    c. Undefined
    d. Undefined

22. In plane geometry, a _____ is a polygon with four equal sides, four right angles, and parallel opposite sides. In algebra, the _____ of a number is that number multiplied by itself.
    a. Square0
    b. Thing
    c. Undefined
    d. Undefined

23. In mathematics, particularly linear algebra, a _____ is a matrix with all its entries being zero.
    a. Thing
    b. Zero matrix0
    c. Undefined
    d. Undefined

24. A _____ can refer to a line joining two nonadjacent vertices of a polygon or polyhedron, or in some contexts any upward or downward sloping line. .
    a. Thing
    b. Diagonal0
    c. Undefined
    d. Undefined

25. _____ is a square matrix in which the entries outside the main diagonal are all zero.
    a. Thing
    b. Diagonal matrix0
    c. Undefined
    d. Undefined

26. _____ element of an element x with respect to a binary operation * with identity element e is an element y such that x * y = y * x = e. In particular,
    a. Inverse0
    b. Thing
    c. Undefined
    d. Undefined

27. In mathematics, the idea of _____ generalises the concepts of negation, in relation to addition, and reciprocal, in relation to multiplication.
    a. Thing
    b. Inverse element0
    c. Undefined
    d. Undefined

28. An _____ is a square matrix which has an inverse.
    a. Thing
    b. Invertible matrix0
    c. Undefined
    d. Undefined

29. In mathematics, a _____ is a demonstration that, assuming certain axioms, some statement is necessarily true.
    a. Thing
    b. Proof0
    c. Undefined
    d. Undefined

30. A _____ consists either of a suggested explanation for a phenomenon or of a reasoned proposal suggesting a possible correlation between multiple phenomena.
    a. Hypothesis0
    b. Thing
    c. Undefined
    d. Undefined

Chapter 1. Matrix Operations

31. A _____ is a symbolic representation denoting a quantity or expression. It often represents an "unknown" quantity that has the potential to change.
    a. Variable0
    b. Thing
    c. Undefined
    d. Undefined

32. A _____ is a first degree polynomial mathematical function of the form: $f(x) = mx + b$ where m and b are real constants and x is a real variable.
    a. Thing
    b. Linear function0
    c. Undefined
    d. Undefined

33. The mathematical concept of a _____ expresses the intuitive idea of deterministic dependence between two quantities, one of which is viewed as primary and the other as secondary. A _____ then is a way to associate a unique output for each input of a specified type, for example, a real number or an element of a given set.
    a. Function0
    b. Thing
    c. Undefined
    d. Undefined

34. The _____ of measurement are a globally standardized and modernized form of the metric system.
    a. Thing
    b. Units0
    c. Undefined
    d. Undefined

35. In mathematics, a _____ is an ordered list of objects. Like a set, it contains members, also called elements or terms, and the number of terms is called the length of the _____. Unlike a set, order matters, and the exact same elements can appear multiple times at different positions in the _____.
    a. Thing
    b. Sequence0
    c. Undefined
    d. Undefined

36. _____ are elementary linear transformations on a matrix which preserve matrix equivalence.
    a. Elementary row operations0
    b. Thing
    c. Undefined
    d. Undefined

37. Elementary _____ are simple transformations which can be applied to a matrix without changing the linear system of equations that it represents.
    a. Row operations0
    b. Thing
    c. Undefined
    d. Undefined

38. In mathematics, _____ refers to the rewriting of an expression into a simpler form.
    a. Thing
    b. Reduction0
    c. Undefined
    d. Undefined

39. _____ is an algorithm which can be used to determine the solutions of a system of linear equations, to find the rank of a matrix, and to calculate the inverse of an invertible square matrix.
    a. Gaussian elimination0
    b. Thing
    c. Undefined
    d. Undefined

40. _____ is an m × 1 matrix, i.e. a matrix consisting of a single column of m elements.

Chapter 1. Matrix Operations

a. Thing
b. Column vector0
c. Undefined
d. Undefined

41. _____ is a set, with some particular properties and usually some additional structure, such as the operations of addition or multiplication, for instance.
    a. Space0
    b. Thing
    c. Undefined
    d. Undefined

42. A _____ is a matrix form used when solving linear systems of equations.
    a. Thing
    b. Row echelon form0
    c. Undefined
    d. Undefined

43. In mathematics, a matrix is in row _____ if is satisfies the following requirements: • All nonzero rows are above any rows of all zeroes. • The leading coefficient of a row is always strictly to the right of the leading coefficient of the row above it.
    a. Thing
    b. Echelon form0
    c. Undefined
    d. Undefined

44. Equivalence is the condition of being _____ or essentially equal.
    a. Equivalent0
    b. Thing
    c. Undefined
    d. Undefined

45. A _____ is a mathematical statement which follows easily from a previously proven statement, typically a mathematical theorem.
    a. Thing
    b. Corollary0
    c. Undefined
    d. Undefined

46. In linear algebra, the _____ of a matrix A is another matrix AT
    a. Transpose0
    b. Thing
    c. Undefined
    d. Undefined

47. A _____ is a four-sided plane figure that has two sets of opposite parallel sides.
    a. Concept
    b. Parallelogram0
    c. Undefined
    d. Undefined

48. In mathematics, _____ is a part of the set theoretic notion of function.
    a. Thing
    b. Image0
    c. Undefined
    d. Undefined

49. In mathematics, the _____ (or modulus) of a real number is its numerical value without regard to its sign.
    a. Absolute value0
    b. Thing
    c. Undefined
    d. Undefined

50. In mathematics, a _____ may be described informally as a number that can be given by an infinite decimal representation.

a. Real number0
b. Thing
c. Undefined
d. Undefined

51. The _____, the average in everyday English, which is also called the arithmetic _____ (and is distinguished from the geometric _____ or harmonic _____). The average is also called the sample _____. The expected value of a random variable, which is also called the population _____.
a. Thing
b. Mean0
c. Undefined
d. Undefined

52. A _____ is 360° or 2∂ radians.
a. Thing
b. Turn0
c. Undefined
d. Undefined

53. An _____ of a product of sums expresses it as a sum of products by using the fact that multiplication distributes over addition.
a. Thing
b. Expansion0
c. Undefined
d. Undefined

54. In linear algebra, a _____ of a matrix A is the determinant of some smaller square matrix, cut down from A.
a. Thing
b. Minor0
c. Undefined
d. Undefined

55. In mathematics, the word _____ is used informally to refer to certain distinct bodies of knowledge about mathematics.
a. Theoretical0
b. Thing
c. Undefined
d. Undefined

56. Mathematical _____ are demonstrations that, assuming certain axioms, some statement is necessarily true.
a. Proofs0
b. Thing
c. Undefined
d. Undefined

57. In mathematics and logic, a _____ proof is a way of showing the truth or falsehood of a given statement by a straightforward combination of established facts, usually existing lemmas and theorems, without making any further assumptions.
a. Direct0
b. Thing
c. Undefined
d. Undefined

58. A _____ of a number is the product of that number with any integer.
a. Multiple0
b. Thing
c. Undefined
d. Undefined

59. In geometry, _____ angles are angles that have a common ray coming out of the vertex going between two other rays.
a. Concept
b. Adjacent0
c. Undefined
d. Undefined

Chapter 1. Matrix Operations

60. In mathematics, a _____ is a statement that can be proved on the basis of explicitly stated or previously agreed assumptions.
    a. Thing
    b. Theorem0
    c. Undefined
    d. Undefined

61. In mathematics, the additive inverse, or _____ of a number n is the number that, when added to n, yields zero. The additive inverse of n is denoted −n. For example, 7 is −7, because 7 + (−7) = 0, and the additive inverse of −0.3 is 0.3, because −0.3 + 0.3 = 0.
    a. Thing
    b. Opposite0
    c. Undefined
    d. Undefined

62. _____ is the rearrangement of objects or symbols into distinguishable sequences.
    a. Thing
    b. Permutation0
    c. Undefined
    d. Undefined

63. In mathematics, the _____ of a number n is the number that, when added to n, yields zero. The _____ of n is denoted −n. For example, 7 is −7, because 7 + (−7) = 0, and the _____ of −0.3 is 0.3, because −0.3 + 0.3 = 0.
    a. Thing
    b. Additive inverse0
    c. Undefined
    d. Undefined

64. A _____ is the result of the addition of a set of numbers. The numbers may be natural numbers, complex numbers, matrices, or still more complicated objects. An infinite _____ is a subtle procedure known as a series.
    a. Thing
    b. Sum0
    c. Undefined
    d. Undefined

65. In mathematics, a _____ is a constant multiplicative factor of a certain object. The object can be such things as a variable, a vector, a function, etc. For example, the _____ of $9x^2$ is 9.
    a. Coefficient0
    b. Thing
    c. Undefined
    d. Undefined

66. In mathematics, a _____ is an expression that is constructed from one or more variables and constants, using only the operations of addition, subtraction, multiplication, and constant positive whole number exponents. is a _____. Note in particular that division by an expression containing a variable is not in general allowed in polynomials. [1]
    a. Polynomial0
    b. Thing
    c. Undefined
    d. Undefined

67. An _____ is a combination of numbers, operators, grouping symbols and/or free variables and bound variables arranged in a meaningful way which can be evaluated..
    a. Expression0
    b. Thing
    c. Undefined
    d. Undefined

68. In mathematics, a _____ is the end result of a division problem. It can also be expressed as the number of times the divisor divides into the dividend.
    a. Thing
    b. Quotient0
    c. Undefined
    d. Undefined

Chapter 1. Matrix Operations

69. A _____ function is a function for which, intuitively, small changes in the input result in small changes in the output.
   a. Continuous0
   b. Event
   c. Undefined
   d. Undefined

70. In chemistry, a _____ is substance made by combining two or more different materials in such a way that no chemical reaction occurs.
   a. Mixture0
   b. Thing
   c. Undefined
   d. Undefined

71. In mathematics, an element x of a ring R is called _____ if there exists some positive integer n such that $x^n = 0$.
   a. Thing
   b. Nilpotent0
   c. Undefined
   d. Undefined

72. In mathematics, factorization (British English: factorisation) or factoring is the decomposition of an object (for example, a number, a polynomial, or a matrix) into a product of other objects, or _____, which when multiplied together give the original.
   a. Thing
   b. Factors0
   c. Undefined
   d. Undefined

73. In mathematics, a _____ is a number in the form of a + bi where a and b are real numbers, and i is the imaginary unit, with the property i 2 = −1. The real number a is called the real part of the _____, and the real number b is the imaginary part.
   a. Complex number0
   b. Thing
   c. Undefined
   d. Undefined

74. In informal language, a _____ is a function that swaps two elements of a set.
   a. Transposition0
   b. Thing
   c. Undefined
   d. Undefined

75. In mathematics, a _____ is an n-tuple with n being 3.
   a. Triple0
   b. Thing
   c. Undefined
   d. Undefined

76. _____ mathematical functions take numeric arguments and produce numeric results.
   a. Miscellaneous0
   b. Thing
   c. Undefined
   d. Undefined

77. Alexandre-Théophile _____ was a French musician and chemist who worked with Bezout and Lavoisier; his name is now principally associated with determinant theory in mathematics. He was born in Paris, and died there.
   a. Vandermonde0
   b. Person
   c. Undefined
   d. Undefined

78. A _____ is a negotiable instrument instructing a financial institution to pay a specific amount of a specific currency from a specific demand account held in the maker/depositor's name with that institution. Both the maker and payee may be natural persons or legal entities.

a. Check0
b. Thing
c. Undefined
d. Undefined

79. In linear algebra, the _____ refers to a matrix consisting of the coefficients of the variables in a set of linear equations.
    a. Coefficient matrix0
    b. Thing
    c. Undefined
    d. Undefined

80. _____ is a special kind of square matrix where the entries below or above the main diagonal are zero.
    a. Thing
    b. Triangular form0
    c. Undefined
    d. Undefined

81. In mathematics, a _____ number is a number which can be expressed as a ratio of two integers. Non-integer _____ numbers (commonly called fractions) are usually written as the vulgar fraction a / b, where b is not zero.
    a. Rational0
    b. Thing
    c. Undefined
    d. Undefined

Chapter 2. Groups

1. An _____ or member of a set is an object that when collected together make up the set.
   a. Thing
   b. Element0
   c. Undefined
   d. Undefined

2. In mathematics, the _____ , or members of a set or more generally a class are all those objects which when collected together make up the set or class.
   a. Thing
   b. Elements0
   c. Undefined
   d. Undefined

3. In mathematics, a _____ of a positive integer n is a way of writing n as a sum of positive integers.
   a. Composition0
   b. Thing
   c. Undefined
   d. Undefined

4. _____ element of an element x with respect to a binary operation * with identity element e is an element y such that x * y = y * x = e. In particular,
   a. Thing
   b. Inverse0
   c. Undefined
   d. Undefined

5. In mathematics, _____ is an elementary arithmetic operation. When one of the numbers is a whole number, _____ is the repeated sum of the other number.
   a. Thing
   b. Multiplication0
   c. Undefined
   d. Undefined

6. In mathematics, a _____ may be described informally as a number that can be given by an infinite decimal representation.
   a. Real number0
   b. Thing
   c. Undefined
   d. Undefined

7. The word _____ comes from the Latin word linearis, which means created by lines.
   a. Thing
   b. Linear0
   c. Undefined
   d. Undefined

8. In mathematics, a _____ is a rectangular table of numbers or, more generally, a table consisting of abstract quantities that can be added and multiplied.
   a. Thing
   b. Matrix0
   c. Undefined
   d. Undefined

9. In mathematics, the idea of _____ generalises the concepts of negation, in relation to addition, and reciprocal, in relation to multiplication.
   a. Thing
   b. Inverse element0
   c. Undefined
   d. Undefined

10. In mathematics, the conjugate _____ or adjoint matrix of an m-by-n matrix A with complex entries is the n-by-m matrix A* obtained from A by taking the transpose and then taking the complex conjugate of each entry.
    a. Pairs0
    b. Thing
    c. Undefined
    d. Undefined

Chapter 2. Groups

11. The _____, the average in everyday English, which is also called the arithmetic _____ (and is distinguished from the geometric _____ or harmonic _____). The average is also called the sample _____. The expected value of a random variable, which is also called the population _____.
    a. Thing
    b. Mean0
    c. Undefined
    d. Undefined

12. In mathematics, a _____ is the result of multiplying, or an expression that identifies factors to be multiplied.
    a. Product0
    b. Thing
    c. Undefined
    d. Undefined

13. Mathematical _____ is used to represent ideas.
    a. Notation0
    b. Thing
    c. Undefined
    d. Undefined

14. In statistics, a _____ measure is one which is measuring what is supposed to measure.
    a. Thing
    b. Valid0
    c. Undefined
    d. Undefined

15. In mathematics, the _____ inverse of a number x, denoted 1/x or x^{-1}, is the number which, when multiplied by x, yields 1. The _____ inverse of x is also called the reciprocal of x.
    a. Multiplicative0
    b. Thing
    c. Undefined
    d. Undefined

16. The _____ is a rule which states that when you add or multiply numbers, changing the order doesn't change the result.
    a. Thing
    b. Commutative law0
    c. Undefined
    d. Undefined

17. In mathematics, the _____ inverse, or opposite, of a number n is the number that, when added to n, yields zero. The _____ inverse of n is denoted −n.
    a. Additive0
    b. Thing
    c. Undefined
    d. Undefined

18. In logic and mathematics, logical _____ is a logical relation that holds between a set T of formulas and a formula B when every model (or interpretation or valuation) of T is also a model of B.
    a. Implication0
    b. Concept
    c. Undefined
    d. Undefined

19. _____ is a property that a binary operation can have.
    a. Thing
    b. Associative law0
    c. Undefined
    d. Undefined

20. In mathematics, the term _____ is applied to certain functions. There are two common ways it is applied: these are related historically, but diverged somewhat during the twentieth century.

Chapter 2. Groups

a. Functional0
b. Thing
c. Undefined
d. Undefined

21. An _____ is an equality that remains true regardless of the values of any variables that appear within it, to distinguish it from an equality which is true under more particular conditions.
    a. Thing
    b. Identity0
    c. Undefined
    d. Undefined

22. In mathematics, the additive inverse, or _____ of a number n is the number that, when added to n, yields zero. The additive inverse of n is denoted −n. For example, 7 is −7, because 7 + (−7) = 0, and the additive inverse of −0.3 is 0.3, because −0.3 + 0.3 = 0.
    a. Thing
    b. Opposite0
    c. Undefined
    d. Undefined

23. In mathematics, the _____ of a number n is the number that, when added to n, yields zero. The _____ of n is denoted −n. For example, 7 is −7, because 7 + (−7) = 0, and the _____ of −0.3 is 0.3, because −0.3 + 0.3 = 0.
    a. Thing
    b. Additive inverse0
    c. Undefined
    d. Undefined

24. In mathematics, a _____ is a demonstration that, assuming certain axioms, some statement is necessarily true.
    a. Proof0
    b. Thing
    c. Undefined
    d. Undefined

25. _____ has many meanings, most of which simply .
    a. Power0
    b. Thing
    c. Undefined
    d. Undefined

26. In mathematics, an _____ (or neutral element) is a special type of element of a set with respect to a binary operation on that set.
    a. Concept
    b. Identity element0
    c. Undefined
    d. Undefined

27. In mathematics, an _____, also called a commutative group, is a group such that a * b= b*a for all and b in G. In other words, the order in which the binary operation is performed doesnt matter.
    a. Thing
    b. Abelian group0
    c. Undefined
    d. Undefined

28. In mathematics, the notion of _____ is a generalization of the notion of invertible.
    a. Cancellation0
    b. Thing
    c. Undefined
    d. Undefined

29. The _____ are the only integral domain whose positive elements are well-ordered, and in which order is preserved by addition. Like the natural numbers, the _____ form a countably infinite set. The set of all _____ is usually denoted in mathematics by a boldface Z .

Chapter 2. Groups

a. Integers0
b. Thing
c. Undefined
d. Undefined

30. _____ is the rearrangement of objects or symbols into distinguishable sequences.
    a. Permutation0
    b. Thing
    c. Undefined
    d. Undefined

31. In informal language, a _____ is a function that swaps two elements of a set.
    a. Thing
    b. Transposition0
    c. Undefined
    d. Undefined

32. The mathematical concept of a _____ expresses the intuitive idea of deterministic dependence between two quantities, one of which is viewed as primary and the other as secondary. A _____ then is a way to associate a unique output for each input of a specified type, for example, a real number or an element of a given set.
    a. Thing
    b. Function0
    c. Undefined
    d. Undefined

33. In group theory, given a group G under a binary operation *, we say that some subset H of G is a _____ of G if H also forms a group under the operation *.
    a. Thing
    b. Subgroup0
    c. Undefined
    d. Undefined

34. A _____ fraction is a fraction in which the absolute value of the numerator is less than the denominator--hence, the absolute value of the fraction is less than 1.
    a. Thing
    b. Proper0
    c. Undefined
    d. Undefined

35. _____ is a circle with a unit radius, i.e., a circle whose radius is 1.
    a. Unit circle0
    b. Thing
    c. Undefined
    d. Undefined

36. In Euclidean geometry, a _____ is the set of all points in a plane at a fixed distance, called the radius, from a given point, the center.
    a. Thing
    b. Circle0
    c. Undefined
    d. Undefined

37. In mathematics, a _____ is a two-dimensional manifold or surface that is perfectly flat.
    a. Plane0
    b. Thing
    c. Undefined
    d. Undefined

38. In mathematics, a _____ is a number in the form of a + bi where a and b are real numbers, and i is the imaginary unit, with the property i 2 = −1. The real number a is called the real part of the _____, and the real number b is the imaginary part.
    a. Thing
    b. Complex number0
    c. Undefined
    d. Undefined

Chapter 2. Groups

39. In mathematics, the _____ (or modulus) of a real number is its numerical value without regard to its sign.
 a. Absolute value0
 b. Thing
 c. Undefined
 d. Undefined

40. An _____ is any starting assumption from which other statements are logically derived
 a. Axiom0
 b. Thing
 c. Undefined
 d. Undefined

41. In mathematics, a _____ of an integer n, also called a factor of n, is an integer which evenly divides n without leaving a remainder.
 a. Divisor0
 b. Thing
 c. Undefined
 d. Undefined

42. In mathematics, the _____ divisor of two non-zero integers, is the largest positive integer that divides both numbers without remainder.
 a. Thing
 b. Greatest common0
 c. Undefined
 d. Undefined

43. In mathematics, a _____ number (or a _____) is a natural number that has exactly two (distinct) natural number divisors, which are 1 and the _____ number itself.
 a. Prime0
 b. Thing
 c. Undefined
 d. Undefined

44. _____ is the state of being greater than any finite real or natural number, however large.
 a. Thing
 b. Infinite0
 c. Undefined
 d. Undefined

45. _____ is the state of being greater than any finite number, however large.
 a. Infinity0
 b. Thing
 c. Undefined
 d. Undefined

46. A _____ is a set whose members are members of another set or a set contained within another set.
 a. Subset0
 b. Thing
 c. Undefined
 d. Undefined

47. A _____ is 360° or 2δ radians.
 a. Thing
 b. Turn0
 c. Undefined
 d. Undefined

48. In mathematics, an _____ (Greek:isos "equal", and morphe "shape") is a bijective map f such that both f and its inverse f $^{-1}$ are homomorphisms, i.e. *structure-preserving* mappings.
 a. Thing
 b. Isomorphism0
 c. Undefined
 d. Undefined

Chapter 2. Groups

49. Two mathematical objects are equal if and only if they are precisely the same in every way. This defines a binary relation, _____, denoted by the sign of _____ "=" in such a way that the statement "x = y" means that x and y are equal.
   a. Equality0
   b. Thing
   c. Undefined
   d. Undefined

50. In mathematics, a _____ of a k-place relation $L \subseteq X_1 \times ... \times X_k$ is one of the sets X_j, $1 \le j \le k$. In the special case where k = 2 and $L \subseteq X_1 \times X_2$ is a function $L : X_1 \to X_2$, it is conventional to refer to X_1 as the _____ of the function and to refer to X_2 as the codomain of the function.
   a. Thing
   b. Domain0
   c. Undefined
   d. Undefined

51. An _____ is a function which does the reverse of a given function.
   a. Inverse function0
   b. Thing
   c. Undefined
   d. Undefined

52. In group theory, a _____ or monogenous group is a group that can be generated by a single element, in the sense that the group has an element g called a "generator" of the group such that, when written multiplicatively, every element of the group is a power of g a multiple of g when the notation is additive.
   a. Cyclic group0
   b. Thing
   c. Undefined
   d. Undefined

53. In set theory and its applications throughout mathematics, _____ are a collection of sets (or sometimes other mathematical objects) that can be unambiguously defined by a property that all its members share.
   a. Thing
   b. Classes0
   c. Undefined
   d. Undefined

54. In mathematics, an _____ is an isomorphism from a mathematical objct of itself while preserving all of its structure.
   a. Automorphism0
   b. Thing
   c. Undefined
   d. Undefined

55. In algebra, a _____ is a binomial formed by taking the opposite of the second term of a binomial.
   a. Thing
   b. Conjugate0
   c. Undefined
   d. Undefined

56. In abstract algebra, a _____ is a structure-preserving map between two algebraic structures. The word _____ comes from the Greek language: homo meaning "same" and morphi meaning "shape".
   a. Thing
   b. Homomorphism0
   c. Undefined
   d. Undefined

57. In category theory and its applications to other branches of mathematics, _____ are a generalization of the kernels of group homomorphisms and the kernels of module homomorphisms and certain other kernels from algebra.
   a. Thing
   b. Kernel0
   c. Undefined
   d. Undefined

58. In mathematics, _____ is a part of the set theoretic notion of function.
   a. Image0
   b. Thing
   c. Undefined
   d. Undefined

59. In algebra, a _____ is a function depending on n that associates a scalar, $det(A)$, to every $n \times n$ square matrix A.
   a. Determinant0
   b. Thing
   c. Undefined
   d. Undefined

60. In geometry, the _____ of an object is a point in some sense in the middle of the object.
   a. Thing
   b. Center0
   c. Undefined
   d. Undefined

61. A _____ is one of the basic shapes of geometry: a polygon with three vertices and three sides which are straight line segments.
   a. Triangle0
   b. Thing
   c. Undefined
   d. Undefined

62. Equivalence is the condition of being _____ or essentially equal.
   a. Equivalent0
   b. Thing
   c. Undefined
   d. Undefined

63. In geometry, two sets are called _____ if one can be transformed into the other by an isometry, i.e., a combination of translations, rotations and reflections.
   a. Congruent0
   b. Thing
   c. Undefined
   d. Undefined

64. In set theory and other branches of mathematics, the _____ of a collection of sets is the set that contains everything that belongs to any of the sets, but nothing else.
   a. Thing
   b. Union0
   c. Undefined
   d. Undefined

65. _____ are groups whose members are members of another set or a set contained within another set.
   a. Subsets0
   b. Thing
   c. Undefined
   d. Undefined

66. Generally, a _____ is a splitting of something into parts.
   a. Thing
   b. Partition0
   c. Undefined
   d. Undefined

67. In mathematics, two sets are said to be _____ if they have no element in common. For example, {1, 2, 3} and {4, 5, 6} are sets which are _____.
   a. Disjoint0
   b. Thing
   c. Undefined
   d. Undefined

68. An _____ is a binary relation between two elements of a set which groups them together as being equivalent in some way.

Chapter 2. Groups

a. Equivalence relation0
b. Thing
c. Undefined
d. Undefined

69. As an abstract term, _____ means similarity between objects.
    a. Thing
    b. Congruence0
    c. Undefined
    d. Undefined

70. In logic, statements p and q are _____ if they have the same logical content.
    a. Thing
    b. Logically equivalent0
    c. Undefined
    d. Undefined

71. Compass and straightedge or ruler-and-compass _____ is the _____ of lengths or angles using only an idealized ruler and compass.
    a. Construction0
    b. Thing
    c. Undefined
    d. Undefined

72. The _____ (symbol _____) and the millibar (symbol mbar, also mb) are units of pressure.
    a. Thing
    b. Bar0
    c. Undefined
    d. Undefined

73. _____ are objects, characters, or other concrete representations of ideas, concepts, or other abstractions.
    a. Symbols0
    b. Thing
    c. Undefined
    d. Undefined

74. A _____ is a mathematical statement which follows easily from a previously proven statement, typically a mathematical theorem.
    a. Thing
    b. Corollary0
    c. Undefined
    d. Undefined

75. A _____ is a negotiable instrument instructing a financial institution to pay a specific amount of a specific currency from a specific demand account held in the maker/depositor's name with that institution. Both the maker and payee may be natural persons or legal entities.
    a. Check0
    b. Thing
    c. Undefined
    d. Undefined

76. In mathematics, if G is a group, H a subgroup of G, and g an element of G, then, gH = {gh : h an element of H} is a left _____ of H in G, and Hg = {hg : h an element of H} is a right _____ of H in G.
    a. Coset0
    b. Thing
    c. Undefined
    d. Undefined

77. The word _____ is used in a variety of ways in mathematics.
    a. Thing
    b. Index0
    c. Undefined
    d. Undefined

78. _____ is the mathematical action of repeatedly adding or subtracting one, usually to find out how many objects there are or to set aside a desired number of objects.

Chapter 2. Groups

a. Counting0
b. Thing
c. Undefined
d. Undefined

79. In mathematics, a _____ is a statement that can be proved on the basis of explicitly stated or previously agreed assumptions.
   a. Theorem0
   b. Thing
   c. Undefined
   d. Undefined

80. In mathematics, a set is called _____ if there is a bijection between the set and some set of the form {1, 2, ..., n} where n is a natural number.
   a. Finite0
   b. Thing
   c. Undefined
   d. Undefined

81. A _____ consists either of a suggested explanation for a phenomenon or of a reasoned proposal suggesting a possible correlation between multiple phenomena.
   a. Thing
   b. Hypothesis0
   c. Undefined
   d. Undefined

82. _____ is that branch of mathematics concerned with the study of groups. These are sets with a rule, or operation. The operation in a group must satisfy closure and have these three additional properties: 1) The operation must have the property of associativity. 2) There must be an identity element. 3) Every element must have a corresponding inverse element. _____ is used throughout mathematics and has several applications in physics and chemistry. Groups can be finite or infinite. A classification of finite simple groups, completed in 1983, is one of the major achievements of mathematics in the 20th century.
   a. Thing
   b. Group theory0
   c. Undefined
   d. Undefined

83. In mathematics, the _____ of two sets A and B is the set that contains all elements of A that also belong to B (or equivalently, all elements of B that also belong to A), but no other elements.
   a. Thing
   b. Intersection0
   c. Undefined
   d. Undefined

84. _____ is the largest positive integer that divides both numbers without remainder.
   a. Common Factor0
   b. Thing
   c. Undefined
   d. Undefined

85. In mathematics, the _____ of a function is the set of all "output" values produced by that function. Given a function $f : A \to B$, the _____ of f, is defined to be the set $\{x \in B : x = f(a)$ for some $a \in A\}$.
   a. Range0
   b. Thing
   c. Undefined
   d. Undefined

86. In mathematics, in the field of group theory, a _____ of a group is a quasisimple subnormal subgroup.
   a. Concept
   b. Component0
   c. Undefined
   d. Undefined

Chapter 2. Groups

87. In mathematics, a _____ is the end result of a division problem. It can also be expressed as the number of times the divisor divides into the dividend.
    a. Thing
    b. Quotient0
    c. Undefined
    d. Undefined

88. A _____ of a number is the product of that number with any integer.
    a. Multiple0
    b. Thing
    c. Undefined
    d. Undefined

89. _____ is a kind of property which exists as magnitude or multitude. It is among the basic classes of things along with quality, substance, change, and relation.
    a. Thing
    b. Amount0
    c. Undefined
    d. Undefined

90. A _____, is a symbolized depiction of space which highlights relations between components of that space. Most usually a _____ is a two-dimensional, geometrically accurate representation of a three-dimensional space.
    a. Map0
    b. Thing
    c. Undefined
    d. Undefined

91. Leonhard _____ was a pioneering Swiss mathematician and physicist, who spent most of his life in Russia and Germany.
    a. Euler0
    b. Person
    c. Undefined
    d. Undefined

92. _____ was a pioneering Swiss mathematician and physicist, who spent most of his life in Russia and Germany.
    a. Person
    b. Leonhard Euler0
    c. Undefined
    d. Undefined

93. An _____ of a number *a* is a number *b* such that $b^n=a$.
    a. Thing
    b. Nth root0
    c. Undefined
    d. Undefined

94. In mathematics, a _____ of a complex-valued function f is a member x of the domain of f such that f(x) vanishes at x, that is, x : f (x) = 0.
    a. Root0
    b. Thing
    c. Undefined
    d. Undefined

95. In mathematics, the nth _____ are all the complex numbers which yield 1 when raised to a given power n. It can be shown that they are located on the unit circle of the complex plane and that in that plane they form the vertices of an n-sided regular polygon with one vertex on 1.
    a. Thing
    b. Roots of unity0
    c. Undefined
    d. Undefined

96. In mathematics and more specifically set theory, the _____ set is the unique set which contains no elements.

20   Chapter 2. Groups

   a. Thing   b. Empty0
   c. Undefined   d. Undefined

97. In mathematics, a _____ is a collection of points which share a property.
   a. Thing   b. Locus0
   c. Undefined   d. Undefined

98. A _____ is an equation in which each term is either a constant or the product of a constant times the first power of a variable.
   a. Linear equation0   b. Thing
   c. Undefined   d. Undefined

99. A _____ can refer to a line joining two nonadjacent vertices of a polygon or polyhedron, or in some contexts any upward or downward sloping line. .
   a. Thing   b. Diagonal0
   c. Undefined   d. Undefined

100. A _____ is the result of the addition of a set of numbers. The numbers may be natural numbers, complex numbers, matrices, or still more complicated objects. An infinite _____ is a subtle procedure known as a series.
   a. Thing   b. Sum0
   c. Undefined   d. Undefined

101. A _____ is the part of the dividend that is left over when the dividend is not evenly divisible by the divisor.
   a. Remainder0   b. Thing
   c. Undefined   d. Undefined

102. _____ in algebra is an application of polynomial long division.
   a. Thing   b. Remainder theorem0
   c. Undefined   d. Undefined

103. The _____ integers are all the integers from zero on upwards.
   a. Thing   b. Nonnegative0
   c. Undefined   d. Undefined

104. _____ is a set, with some particular properties and usually some additional structure, such as the operations of addition or multiplication, for instance.
   a. Space0   b. Thing
   c. Undefined   d. Undefined

105. A _____ function is a function for which, intuitively, small changes in the input result in small changes in the output.
   a. Event   b. Continuous0
   c. Undefined   d. Undefined

106. In elementary algebra, an _____ is a set that contains every real number between two indicated numbers and may contain the two numbers themselves.

a. Interval0
c. Undefined
b. Thing
d. Undefined

Chapter 3. Vector Spaces

1. In mathematics, _____ is an elementary arithmetic operation. When one of the numbers is a whole number, _____ is the repeated sum of the other number.
   - a. Thing
   - b. Multiplication0
   - c. Undefined
   - d. Undefined

2. In physics and in _____ calculus, a spatial _____, or simply _____, is a concept characterized by a magnitude and a direction.
   - a. Thing
   - b. Vector0
   - c. Undefined
   - d. Undefined

3. _____ is a collection of objects called vectors that, informally speaking, may be scaled and added.
   - a. Thing
   - b. Vector space0
   - c. Undefined
   - d. Undefined

4. _____ is a set, with some particular properties and usually some additional structure, such as the operations of addition or multiplication, for instance.
   - a. Space0
   - b. Thing
   - c. Undefined
   - d. Undefined

5. In mathematics, a matrix can be thought of as each row or _____ being a vector. Hence, a space formed by row vectors or _____ vectors are said to be a row space or a _____ space.
   - a. Column0
   - b. Concept
   - c. Undefined
   - d. Undefined

6. _____ is an m × 1 matrix, i.e. a matrix consisting of a single column of m elements.
   - a. Column vector0
   - b. Thing
   - c. Undefined
   - d. Undefined

7. _____ was a German mathematician, recognized as one of the most influential and universal mathematicians of the 19th and early 20th centuries. He invented or developed a broad range of fundamental ideas, in invariant theory, the axiomatization of geometry, and with the notion of Hilbert space, one of the foundations of functional analysis.
   - a. David Hilbert0
   - b. Person
   - c. Undefined
   - d. Undefined

8. In mathematics, a _____ is a rectangular table of numbers or, more generally, a table consisting of abstract quantities that can be added and multiplied.
   - a. Thing
   - b. Matrix0
   - c. Undefined
   - d. Undefined

9. In linear algebra, a _____ is a 1 × n matrix, that is, a matrix consisting of a single row
   - a. Row vector0
   - b. Thing
   - c. Undefined
   - d. Undefined

10. In linear algebra and related areas of mathematics, the null vector or _____ is the vector in Euclidean space, all of whose components are zero.

Chapter 3. Vector Spaces

a. Zero vector0
b. Thing
c. Undefined
d. Undefined

11. In mathematics, the _____ of a coordinate system is the point where the axes of the system intersect.
a. Origin0
b. Thing
c. Undefined
d. Undefined

12. A _____ is a four-sided plane figure that has two sets of opposite parallel sides.
a. Parallelogram0
b. Concept
c. Undefined
d. Undefined

13. In combinatorial mathematics, a _____ is an un-ordered collection of unique elements.
a. Concept
b. Combination0
c. Undefined
d. Undefined

14. The word _____ comes from the Latin word linearis, which means created by lines.
a. Thing
b. Linear0
c. Undefined
d. Undefined

15. In linear algebra, real numbers are called scalars and relate to vectors in a vector space through the operation of _____ multiplication, in which a vector can be multiplied by a number to produce another vector.
a. Thing
b. Scalar0
c. Undefined
d. Undefined

16. Equivalence is the condition of being _____ or essentially equal.
a. Equivalent0
b. Thing
c. Undefined
d. Undefined

17. In mathematics, a _____ may be described informally as a number that can be given by an infinite decimal representation.
a. Thing
b. Real number0
c. Undefined
d. Undefined

18. _____ is one of the basic operations defining a vector space in linear algebra.
a. Scalar multiplication0
b. Thing
c. Undefined
d. Undefined

19. In mathematics, a _____ of a positive integer n is a way of writing n as a sum of positive integers.
a. Composition0
b. Thing
c. Undefined
d. Undefined

20. In mathematics, a _____ is the result of multiplying, or an expression that identifies factors to be multiplied.
a. Product0
b. Thing
c. Undefined
d. Undefined

Chapter 3. Vector Spaces

21. _____ is a binary operation on two vectors in a three-dimensional Euclidean space that results in another vector which is perpedicular to the two input vectors.
   a. Thing
   b. Cross product0
   c. Undefined
   d. Undefined

22. The _____, the average in everyday English, which is also called the arithmetic _____ (and is distinguished from the geometric _____ or harmonic _____). The average is also called the sample _____. The expected value of a random variable, which is also called the population _____.
   a. Mean0
   b. Thing
   c. Undefined
   d. Undefined

23. The _____ relates to the binary operation of multiplication and addition.
   a. Thing
   b. Distributive law0
   c. Undefined
   d. Undefined

24. In mathematics, a _____ is a number in the form of a + bi where a and b are real numbers, and i is the imaginary unit, with the property i 2 = −1. The real number a is called the real part of the _____, and the real number b is the imaginary part.
   a. Thing
   b. Complex number0
   c. Undefined
   d. Undefined

25. In mathematics, a _____ is an expression that is constructed from one or more variables and constants, using only the operations of addition, subtraction, multiplication, and constant positive whole number exponents. is a _____. Note in particular that division by an expression containing a variable is not in general allowed in polynomials. [1]
   a. Polynomial0
   b. Thing
   c. Undefined
   d. Undefined

26. A _____ function is a function for which, intuitively, small changes in the input result in small changes in the output.
   a. Continuous0
   b. Event
   c. Undefined
   d. Undefined

27. The mathematical concept of a _____ expresses the intuitive idea of deterministic dependence between two quantities, one of which is viewed as primary and the other as secondary. A _____ then is a way to associate a unique output for each input of a specified type, for example, a real number or an element of a given set.
   a. Function0
   b. Thing
   c. Undefined
   d. Undefined

28. In elementary algebra, an _____ is a set that contains every real number between two indicated numbers and may contain the two numbers themselves.
   a. Thing
   b. Interval0
   c. Undefined
   d. Undefined

29. In geographic information systems, a _____ comprises an entity with a geographic location, typically determined by points, arcs, or polygons. Carriageways and cadastres exemplify _____ data.

Chapter 3. Vector Spaces

a. Feature0
b. Thing
c. Undefined
d. Undefined

30. _____ is a branch of mathematics concerning the study of structure, relation and quantity.
    a. Concept
    b. Algebra0
    c. Undefined
    d. Undefined

31. A _____ is a negotiable instrument instructing a financial institution to pay a specific amount of a specific currency from a specific demand account held in the maker/depositor's name with that institution. Both the maker and payee may be natural persons or legal entities.
    a. Thing
    b. Check0
    c. Undefined
    d. Undefined

32. In mathematics, a _____ number is a number which can be expressed as a ratio of two integers. Non-integer _____ numbers (commonly called fractions) are usually written as the vulgar fraction a / b, where b is not zero.
    a. Rational0
    b. Thing
    c. Undefined
    d. Undefined

33. An _____ is any starting assumption from which other statements are logically derived
    a. Thing
    b. Axiom0
    c. Undefined
    d. Undefined

34. The _____ are the only integral domain whose positive elements are well-ordered, and in which order is preserved by addition. Like the natural numbers, the _____ form a countably infinite set. The set of all _____ is usually denoted in mathematics by a boldface Z .
    a. Thing
    b. Integers0
    c. Undefined
    d. Undefined

35. In set theory and its applications throughout mathematics, _____ are a collection of sets (or sometimes other mathematical objects) that can be unambiguously defined by a property that all its members share.
    a. Thing
    b. Classes0
    c. Undefined
    d. Undefined

36. In mathematics, a set is called _____ if there is a bijection between the set and some set of the form {1, 2, ..., n} where n is a natural number.
    a. Thing
    b. Finite0
    c. Undefined
    d. Undefined

37. An _____ or member of a set is an object that when collected together make up the set.
    a. Element0
    b. Thing
    c. Undefined
    d. Undefined

38. An _____ is an equality that remains true regardless of the values of any variables that appear within it, to distinguish it from an equality which is true under more particular conditions.

Chapter 3. Vector Spaces

    a. Thing   b. Identity0
    c. Undefined   d. Undefined

39. In mathematics, an _____ (or neutral element) is a special type of element of a set with respect to a binary operation on that set.
   a. Identity element0   b. Concept
   c. Undefined   d. Undefined

40. In mathematics, the _____ inverse of a number x, denoted 1/x or x^{-1}, is the number which, when multiplied by x, yields 1. The _____ inverse of x is also called the reciprocal of x.
   a. Thing   b. Multiplicative0
   c. Undefined   d. Undefined

41. _____ element of an element x with respect to a binary operation * with identity element e is an element y such that x * y = y * x = e. In particular,
   a. Thing   b. Inverse0
   c. Undefined   d. Undefined

42. In mathematics, a _____ number (or a _____) is a natural number that has exactly two (distinct) natural number divisors, which are 1 and the _____ number itself.
   a. Prime0   b. Thing
   c. Undefined   d. Undefined

43. As an abstract term, _____ means similarity between objects.
   a. Thing   b. Congruence0
   c. Undefined   d. Undefined

44. In geometry, two sets are called _____ if one can be transformed into the other by an isometry, i.e., a combination of translations, rotations and reflections.
   a. Thing   b. Congruent0
   c. Undefined   d. Undefined

45. In mathematics, the _____, or members of a set or more generally a class are all those objects which when collected together make up the set or class.
   a. Elements0   b. Thing
   c. Undefined   d. Undefined

46. In mathematics, the notion of _____ is a generalization of the notion of invertible.
   a. Cancellation0   b. Thing
   c. Undefined   d. Undefined

47. In mathematics, the _____ divisor of two non-zero integers, is the largest positive integer that divides both numbers without remainder.
   a. Thing   b. Greatest common0
   c. Undefined   d. Undefined

Chapter 3. Vector Spaces

48. In mathematics, a _____ of an integer n, also called a factor of n, is an integer which evenly divides n without leaving a remainder.
    a. Thing
    b. Divisor0
    c. Undefined
    d. Undefined

49. Two mathematical objects are equal if and only if they are precisely the same in every way. This defines a binary relation, _____, denoted by the sign of _____ "=" in such a way that the statement "x = y" means that x and y are equal.
    a. Thing
    b. Equality0
    c. Undefined
    d. Undefined

50. A _____ is a mathematical statement which follows easily from a previously proven statement, typically a mathematical theorem.
    a. Corollary0
    b. Thing
    c. Undefined
    d. Undefined

51. In mathematics, a _____ is a constant multiplicative factor of a certain object. The object can be such things as a variable, a vector, a function, etc. For example, the _____ of $9x^2$ is 9.
    a. Coefficient0
    b. Thing
    c. Undefined
    d. Undefined

52. In algebra, a _____ is a function depending on n that associates a scalar, det(A), to every $n \times n$ square matrix A.
    a. Thing
    b. Determinant0
    c. Undefined
    d. Undefined

53. In mathematics, the idea of _____ generalises the concepts of negation, in relation to addition, and reciprocal, in relation to multiplication.
    a. Inverse element0
    b. Thing
    c. Undefined
    d. Undefined

54. A _____ is a set whose members are members of another set or a set contained within another set.
    a. Thing
    b. Subset0
    c. Undefined
    d. Undefined

55. In mathematics, an _____ (Greek:isos "equal", and morphe "shape") is a bijective map f such that both f and its inverse f â¨1 are homomorphisms, i.e. *structure-preserving* mappings.
    a. Thing
    b. Isomorphism0
    c. Undefined
    d. Undefined

56. Order theory is a branch of mathematics that studies various kinds of binary relations that capture the intuitive notion of a mathematical _____.
    a. Ordering0
    b. Thing
    c. Undefined
    d. Undefined

57. _____ is the state of being greater than any finite real or natural number, however large.

Chapter 3. Vector Spaces

a. Thing
b. Infinite0
c. Undefined
d. Undefined

58. In set theory, an _____ is a set that is not a finite set. Infinite sets may be countable or uncountable.
a. Thing
b. Infinite set0
c. Undefined
d. Undefined

59. A _____ is an equation in which each term is either a constant or the product of a constant times the first power of a variable.
a. Linear equation0
b. Thing
c. Undefined
d. Undefined

60. A _____ of a number is the product of that number with any integer.
a. Multiple0
b. Thing
c. Undefined
d. Undefined

61. In mathematics, a _____ is a demonstration that, assuming certain axioms, some statement is necessarily true.
a. Thing
b. Proof0
c. Undefined
d. Undefined

62. _____ also called natural basis or canonical basis of the n-dimensional Euclidean space Rn is the basis obtained by taking the n basis vectors
a. Standard basis0
b. Thing
c. Undefined
d. Undefined

63. In mathematics, a _____ occurs if there is a bijection between the set and some set of the form 1, 2, ..., n where n is a natural number.
a. Concept
b. Finite set0
c. Undefined
d. Undefined

64. In mathematics and more specifically set theory, the _____ set is the unique set which contains no elements.
a. Empty0
b. Thing
c. Undefined
d. Undefined

65. _____ are groups whose members are members of another set or a set contained within another set.
a. Thing
b. Subsets0
c. Undefined
d. Undefined

66. A _____ is the result of the addition of a set of numbers. The numbers may be natural numbers, complex numbers, matrices, or still more complicated objects. An infinite _____ is a subtle procedure known as a series.
a. Thing
b. Sum0
c. Undefined
d. Undefined

67. A _____ is a set of numbers that designate location in a given reference system, such as x,y in a planar _____ system or an x,y,z in a three-dimensional _____ system.

Chapter 3. Vector Spaces

    a. Thing
    c. Undefined
    b. Coordinate0
    d. Undefined

68. An _____ is a square matrix which has an inverse.
    a. Thing
    c. Undefined
    b. Invertible matrix0
    d. Undefined

69. Mathematical _____ is used to represent ideas.
    a. Thing
    c. Undefined
    b. Notation0
    d. Undefined

70. In mathematics, a subset of Euclidean space R^n is called _____ if it is closed and bounded.
    a. Compact0
    c. Undefined
    b. Thing
    d. Undefined

71. In common philosophical language, a proposition or _____, is the content of an assertion, that is, it is true-or-false and defined by the meaning of a particular piece of language.
    a. Statement0
    c. Undefined
    b. Concept
    d. Undefined

72. In mathematics, a _____ is an ordered list of objects. Like a set, it contains members, also called elements or terms, and the number of terms is called the length of the _____. Unlike a set, order matters, and the exact same elements can appear multiple times at different positions in the _____.
    a. Thing
    c. Undefined
    b. Sequence0
    d. Undefined

73. In mathematics, _____ describes an entity with a limit.
    a. Convergent0
    c. Undefined
    b. Thing
    d. Undefined

74. In mathematical analysis and related areas of mathematics, a set is called _____, if it is, in a certain sense, of finite size.
    a. Bounded0
    c. Undefined
    b. Thing
    d. Undefined

75. A _____ is the sum of the elements of a sequence.
    a. Series0
    c. Undefined
    b. Thing
    d. Undefined

76. _____ a series is the sum of the terms of a sequence of numbers.
    a. Convergent series0
    c. Undefined
    b. Thing
    d. Undefined

77. _____ or integral is said to converge absolutely if the sum or integral of the absolute value of the summand or integrand is finite.

Chapter 3. Vector Spaces

a. Thing
b. Absolutely convergent series0
c. Undefined
d. Undefined

78. In mathematics and logic, a _____ proof is a way of showing the truth or falsehood of a given statement by a straightforward combination of established facts, usually existing lemmas and theorems, without making any further assumptions.
a. Thing
b. Direct0
c. Undefined
d. Undefined

79. In mathematics, the _____ of two sets A and B is the set that contains all elements of A that also belong to B (or equivalently, all elements of B that also belong to A), but no other elements.
a. Thing
b. Intersection0
c. Undefined
d. Undefined

80. Statistical _____ is a statistical procedure in which individual items are placed into groups based on quantitative information on one or more characteristics inherent in the items and based on a training set of previously labeled items.
a. Thing
b. Classification0
c. Undefined
d. Undefined

81. In group theory, given a group G under a binary operation *, we say that some subset H of G is a _____ of G if H also forms a group under the operation *.
a. Thing
b. Subgroup0
c. Undefined
d. Undefined

82. In abstract algebra, a _____ is a structure-preserving map between two algebraic structures. The word _____ comes from the Greek language: homo meaning "same" and morphi meaning "shape".
a. Thing
b. Homomorphism0
c. Undefined
d. Undefined

83. In mathematics, a _____ is a statement that can be proved on the basis of explicitly stated or previously agreed assumptions.
a. Thing
b. Theorem0
c. Undefined
d. Undefined

84. In plane geometry, a _____ is a polygon with four equal sides, four right angles, and parallel opposite sides. In algebra, the _____ of a number is that number multiplied by itself.
a. Square0
b. Thing
c. Undefined
d. Undefined

85. In linear algebra, the _____ of an n-by-n square matrix A is defined to be the sum of the elements on the main diagonal of A,
a. Trace0
b. Thing
c. Undefined
d. Undefined

86. A _____ fraction is a fraction in which the absolute value of the numerator is less than the denominator--hence, the absolute value of the fraction is less than 1.

Chapter 3. Vector Spaces

a. Thing
b. Proper0
c. Undefined
d. Undefined

87. In set theory and other branches of mathematics, the _____ of a collection of sets is the set that contains everything that belongs to any of the sets, but nothing else.
 a. Union0
 b. Thing
 c. Undefined
 d. Undefined

88. In mathematics, a _____ is a polynomial equation of the second degree. The general form is $ax^2 + bx + c = 0$.
 a. Quadratic equation0
 b. Thing
 c. Undefined
 d. Undefined

89. The _____ of a ring R is defined to be the smallest positive integer n such that $n\,a = 0$, for all a in R.
 a. Thing
 b. Characteristic0
 c. Undefined
 d. Undefined

90. _____ of a polynomial with real or complex coefficients is a certain expression in the coefficients of the polynomial which is equal to zero if and only if the polynomial has a multiple root i.e. a root with multiplicity greater than one in the complex numbers.
 a. Discriminant0
 b. Thing
 c. Undefined
 d. Undefined

91. In mathematics, a _____ of a complex-valued function f is a member x of the domain of f such that f(x) vanishes at x, that is, x : f (x) = 0.
 a. Thing
 b. Root0
 c. Undefined
 d. Undefined

92. A _____ is a symbolic representation denoting a quantity or expression. It often represents an "unknown" quantity that has the potential to change.
 a. Thing
 b. Variable0
 c. Undefined
 d. Undefined

93. In mathematics, the concept of a _____ tries to capture the intuitive idea of a geometrical one-dimensional and continuous object. A simple example is the circle.
 a. Thing
 b. Curve0
 c. Undefined
 d. Undefined

94. In mathematics, a _____ is a collection of points which share a property.
 a. Thing
 b. Locus0
 c. Undefined
 d. Undefined

Chapter 4. Linear Transformations

1. In mathematics, a _____ in elementary terms is any of a variety of different functions from geometry, such as rotations, reflections and translations.
   a. Transformation0
   b. Thing
   c. Undefined
   d. Undefined

2. The word _____ comes from the Latin word linearis, which means created by lines.
   a. Thing
   b. Linear0
   c. Undefined
   d. Undefined

3. In mathematics, a linear map also called a _____ or linear operator is a function between two vector spaces that preserves the operations of vector addition and scalar multiplication.
   a. Thing
   b. Linear transformation0
   c. Undefined
   d. Undefined

4. The _____ is a measurement of how a function changes when the values of its inputs change.
   a. Derivative0
   b. Thing
   c. Undefined
   d. Undefined

5. In mathematics, _____ is an elementary arithmetic operation. When one of the numbers is a whole number, _____ is the repeated sum of the other number.
   a. Multiplication0
   b. Thing
   c. Undefined
   d. Undefined

6. In physics and in _____ calculus, a spatial _____, or simply _____, is a concept characterized by a magnitude and a direction.
   a. Thing
   b. Vector0
   c. Undefined
   d. Undefined

7. In category theory and its applications to other branches of mathematics, _____ are a generalization of the kernels of group homomorphisms and the kernels of module homomorphisms and certain other kernels from algebra.
   a. Thing
   b. Kernel0
   c. Undefined
   d. Undefined

8. In mathematics, _____ is a part of the set theoretic notion of function.
   a. Thing
   b. Image0
   c. Undefined
   d. Undefined

9. A _____ is an equation in which each term is either a constant or the product of a constant times the first power of a variable.
   a. Thing
   b. Linear equation0
   c. Undefined
   d. Undefined

10. In mathematics, a _____ is a rectangular table of numbers or, more generally, a table consisting of abstract quantities that can be added and multiplied.
    a. Thing
    b. Matrix0
    c. Undefined
    d. Undefined

Chapter 4. Linear Transformations

11. In mathematics, a _____ is a statement that can be proved on the basis of explicitly stated or previously agreed assumptions.
    a. Theorem0
    b. Thing
    c. Undefined
    d. Undefined

12. In mathematics, a set is called _____ if there is a bijection between the set and some set of the form {1, 2, ..., n} where n is a natural number.
    a. Finite0
    b. Thing
    c. Undefined
    d. Undefined

13. In mathematics, if G is a group, H a subgroup of G, and g an element of G, then, gH = {gh : h an element of H } is a left _____ of H in G, and Hg = {hg : h an element of H } is a right _____ of H in G.
    a. Coset0
    b. Thing
    c. Undefined
    d. Undefined

14. _____ is a set, with some particular properties and usually some additional structure, such as the operations of addition or multiplication, for instance.
    a. Thing
    b. Space0
    c. Undefined
    d. Undefined

15. In mathematics, the _____ inverse, or opposite, of a number n is the number that, when added to n, yields zero. The _____ inverse of n is denoted −n.
    a. Additive0
    b. Thing
    c. Undefined
    d. Undefined

16. A _____ is a set of numbers that designate location in a given reference system, such as x,y in a planar _____ system or an x,y,z in a three-dimensional _____ system.
    a. Thing
    b. Coordinate0
    c. Undefined
    d. Undefined

17. _____ is a collection of objects called vectors that, informally speaking, may be scaled and added.
    a. Vector space0
    b. Thing
    c. Undefined
    d. Undefined

18. In plane geometry, a _____ is a polygon with four equal sides, four right angles, and parallel opposite sides. In algebra, the _____ of a number is that number multiplied by itself.
    a. Thing
    b. Square0
    c. Undefined
    d. Undefined

19. In mathematics, the idea of _____ generalises the concepts of negation, in relation to addition, and reciprocal, in relation to multiplication.
    a. Inverse element0
    b. Thing
    c. Undefined
    d. Undefined

20. An _____ is an equality that remains true regardless of the values of any variables that appear within it, to distinguish it from an equality which is true under more particular conditions.

Chapter 4. Linear Transformations

- a. Thing
- b. Identity0
- c. Undefined
- d. Undefined

21. _____ is a kind of property which exists as magnitude or multitude. It is among the basic classes of things along with quality, substance, change, and relation.
    - a. Amount0
    - b. Thing
    - c. Undefined
    - d. Undefined

22. In mathematics, a matrix can be thought of as each row or _____ being a vector. Hence, a space formed by row vectors or _____ vectors are said to be a row space or a _____ space.
    - a. Concept
    - b. Column0
    - c. Undefined
    - d. Undefined

23. Elementary _____ are simple transformations which can be applied to a matrix without changing the linear system of equations that it represents.
    - a. Thing
    - b. Row operations0
    - c. Undefined
    - d. Undefined

24. In mathematics, a _____ is a demonstration that, assuming certain axioms, some statement is necessarily true.
    - a. Proof0
    - b. Thing
    - c. Undefined
    - d. Undefined

25. _____ has many meanings, most of which simply .
    - a. Power0
    - b. Thing
    - c. Undefined
    - d. Undefined

26. In mathematics and its applications, a _____ is a system for assigning an n-tuple of numbers or scalars to each point in an n-dimensional space.
    - a. Concept
    - b. Coordinate system0
    - c. Undefined
    - d. Undefined

27. In mathematics and its applications, _____ are used for assigning an n-tuple of numbers or scalars to each point in an n-dimensional space.
    - a. Coordinate systems0
    - b. Concept
    - c. Undefined
    - d. Undefined

28. A frame of _____ is a particular perspective from which the universe is observed.
    - a. Reference0
    - b. Thing
    - c. Undefined
    - d. Undefined

29. In algebra, a _____ is a binomial formed by taking the opposite of the second term of a binomial.
    - a. Thing
    - b. Conjugate0
    - c. Undefined
    - d. Undefined

30. An _____ of a linear transformation is a non-zero vector that is either left unaffected or simply multiplied by a scale factor after the transformation.

Chapter 4. Linear Transformations

a. Thing
c. Undefined
b. Eigenvector0
d. Undefined

31. In mathematics, an _____ is something that does not change under a set of transformations. The property of being an _____ is invariance.
   a. Thing
   c. Undefined
   b. Invariant0
   d. Undefined

32. In linear algebra, real numbers are called scalars and relate to vectors in a vector space through the operation of _____ multiplication, in which a vector can be multiplied by a number to produce another vector.
   a. Thing
   c. Undefined
   b. Scalar0
   d. Undefined

33. A vector can be thought of as an arrow. It has a length, called its magnitude, and it points in some particular direction. A linear transformation inputs a vector and changes it, usually changing both its magnitude and its direction. An eigenvector of a given linear transformation is a vector which is simply multiplied by a constant called the _____ during that transformation.
   a. Eigenvalue0
   c. Undefined
   b. Thing
   d. Undefined

34. The _____, the average in everyday English, which is also called the arithmetic _____ (and is distinguished from the geometric _____ or harmonic _____). The average is also called the sample _____. The expected value of a random variable, which is also called the population _____.
   a. Thing
   c. Undefined
   b. Mean0
   d. Undefined

35. A _____ can refer to a line joining two nonadjacent vertices of a polygon or polyhedron, or in some contexts any upward or downward sloping line. .
   a. Thing
   c. Undefined
   b. Diagonal0
   d. Undefined

36. _____ is a square matrix in which the entries outside the main diagonal are all zero.
   a. Diagonal matrix0
   c. Undefined
   b. Thing
   d. Undefined

37. A circular _____ or circle _____ also known as a pie piece is the portion of a circle enclosed by two radii and an arc.
   a. Sector0
   c. Undefined
   b. Thing
   d. Undefined

38. A _____ consists of one quarter of the coordinate plane.
   a. Quadrant0
   c. Undefined
   b. Thing
   d. Undefined

39. A _____ is a four-sided plane figure that has two sets of opposite parallel sides.

Chapter 4. Linear Transformations

    a. Parallelogram0   b. Concept
    c. Undefined   d. Undefined

40. In mathematical analysis and related areas of mathematics, a set is called _____, if it is, in a certain sense, of finite size.
    a. Thing   b. Bounded0
    c. Undefined   d. Undefined

41. In mathematics, the _____ of two sets A and B is the set that contains all elements of A that also belong to B (or equivalently, all elements of B that also belong to A), but no other elements.
    a. Thing   b. Intersection0
    c. Undefined   d. Undefined

42. A _____ is 360° or 2δ radians.
    a. Thing   b. Turn0
    c. Undefined   d. Undefined

43. An _____ is a square matrix which has an inverse.
    a. Thing   b. Invertible matrix0
    c. Undefined   d. Undefined

44. In mathematics, an _____ (Greek:isos "equal", and morphe "shape") is a bijective map f such that both f and its inverse f^{-1} are homomorphisms, i.e. *structure-preserving* mappings.
    a. Isomorphism0   b. Thing
    c. Undefined   d. Undefined

45. Equivalence is the condition of being _____ or essentially equal.
    a. Equivalent0   b. Thing
    c. Undefined   d. Undefined

46. In algebra, a _____ is a function depending on n that associates a scalar, det(A), to every $n \times n$ square matrix A.
    a. Thing   b. Determinant0
    c. Undefined   d. Undefined

47. A _____ is a symbolic representation denoting a quantity or expression. It often represents an "unknown" quantity that has the potential to change.
    a. Thing   b. Variable0
    c. Undefined   d. Undefined

48. The _____ of a ring R is defined to be the smallest positive integer n such that $n\,a = 0$, for all a in R.
    a. Characteristic0   b. Thing
    c. Undefined   d. Undefined

49. In mathematics, a _____ is an expression that is constructed from one or more variables and constants, using only the operations of addition, subtraction, multiplication, and constant positive whole number exponents. is a _____. Note in particular that division by an expression containing a variable is not in general allowed in polynomials. [1]

Chapter 4. Linear Transformations

a. Polynomial0
c. Undefined
b. Thing
d. Undefined

50. A _____ is a mathematical statement which follows easily from a previously proven statement, typically a mathematical theorem.
a. Thing
c. Undefined
b. Corollary0
d. Undefined

51. In mathematics, a _____ of a complex-valued function f is a member x of the domain of f such that f(x) vanishes at x, that is, x : f (x) = 0.
a. Thing
c. Undefined
b. Root0
d. Undefined

52. _____ is a special kind of square matrix where the entries below or above the main diagonal are zero.
a. Thing
c. Undefined
b. Triangular form0
d. Undefined

53. In mathematics, a _____ is the result of multiplying, or an expression that identifies factors to be multiplied.
a. Thing
c. Undefined
b. Product0
d. Undefined

54. _____ of a polynomial with real or complex coefficients is a certain expression in the coefficients of the polynomial which is equal to zero if and only if the polynomial has a multiple root i.e. a root with multiplicity greater than one in the complex numbers.
a. Thing
c. Undefined
b. Discriminant0
d. Undefined

55. In mathematics, a _____ may be described informally as a number that can be given by an infinite decimal representation.
a. Thing
c. Undefined
b. Real number0
d. Undefined

56. In linear algebra, the _____ of an n-by-n square matrix A is defined to be the sum of the elements on the main diagonal of A,
a. Trace0
c. Undefined
b. Thing
d. Undefined

57. A _____ is the result of the addition of a set of numbers. The numbers may be natural numbers, complex numbers, matrices, or still more complicated objects. An infinite _____ is a subtle procedure known as a series.
a. Sum0
c. Undefined
b. Thing
d. Undefined

58. In mathematics, a _____ is a constant multiplicative factor of a certain object. The object can be such things as a variable, a vector, a function, etc. For example, the _____ of $9x^2$ is 9.

Chapter 4. Linear Transformations

a. Thing
b. Coefficient0
c. Undefined
d. Undefined

59. In mathematics, a _____ is a number in the form of a + bi where a and b are real numbers, and i is the imaginary unit, with the property i 2 = −1. The real number a is called the real part of the _____, and the real number b is the imaginary part.
   a. Complex number0
   b. Thing
   c. Undefined
   d. Undefined

60. In mathematics, there are several meanings of _____ depending on the subject.
   a. Thing
   b. Degree0
   c. Undefined
   d. Undefined

61. A _____ is a movement of an object in a circular motion. A two-dimensional object rotates around a center (or point) of _____. A three-dimensional object rotates around a line called an axis. If the axis of _____ is within the body, the body is said to rotate upon itself, or spin—which implies relative speed and perhaps free-movement with angular momentum. A circular motion about an external point, e.g. the Earth about the Sun, is called an orbit or more properly an orbital revolution.
   a. Rotation0
   b. Thing
   c. Undefined
   d. Undefined

62. In mathematics, a _____ is a two-dimensional manifold or surface that is perfectly flat.
   a. Thing
   b. Plane0
   c. Undefined
   d. Undefined

63. In mathematics, the conjugate _____ or adjoint matrix of an m-by-n matrix A with complex entries is the n-by-m matrix A* obtained from A by taking the transpose and then taking the complex conjugate of each entry.
   a. Pairs0
   b. Thing
   c. Undefined
   d. Undefined

64. In group theory, given a group G under a binary operation *, we say that some subset H of G is a _____ of G if H also forms a group under the operation *.
   a. Subgroup0
   b. Thing
   c. Undefined
   d. Undefined

65. In mathematics, _____ is synonymous with perpendicular when used as a simple adjective that is not part of any longer phrase with a standard definition. It means at right angles. It comes from the Greek á½€Ï Î¸ÏŒÏ, orthos, meaning "straight", used by Euclid to mean right; and Î³Ï‰Î½Î¯Î± gonia, meaning angle. Two streets that cross each other at a right angle are _____ to one another.
   a. Orthogonal0
   b. Thing
   c. Undefined
   d. Undefined

66. An _____ or member of a set is an object that when collected together make up the set.
   a. Thing
   b. Element0
   c. Undefined
   d. Undefined

Chapter 4. Linear Transformations

67. In mathematics, the _____ , or members of a set or more generally a class are all those objects which when collected together make up the set or class.
    a. Thing
    b. Elements0
    c. Undefined
    d. Undefined

68. The word _____ is used in a variety of ways in mathematics.
    a. Index0
    b. Thing
    c. Undefined
    d. Undefined

69. In mathematics, the _____ of a coordinate system is the point where the axes of the system intersect.
    a. Origin0
    b. Thing
    c. Undefined
    d. Undefined

70. In mathematics, a _____ of a positive integer n is a way of writing n as a sum of positive integers.
    a. Composition0
    b. Thing
    c. Undefined
    d. Undefined

71. The _____ functions is determined by the nesting of two or more functions to form a single new function.
    a. Thing
    b. Composition of two0
    c. Undefined
    d. Undefined

72. An _____ is a straight line around which a geometric figure can be rotated.
    a. Axis0
    b. Thing
    c. Undefined
    d. Undefined

73. _____ is the study of terms and their use — of words and compound words that are used in specific contexts.
    a. Terminology0
    b. Thing
    c. Undefined
    d. Undefined

74. In mathematics, the _____, also known as the scalar product, is a binary operation which takes two vectors over the real numbers R and returns a real-valued scalar quantity. It is the standard inner product of the Euclidean space.
    a. Thing
    b. Dot product0
    c. Undefined
    d. Undefined

75. _____ is an m × 1 matrix, i.e. a matrix consisting of a single column of m elements.
    a. Thing
    b. Column vector0
    c. Undefined
    d. Undefined

76. A _____ is one of the basic shapes of geometry: a polygon with three vertices and three sides which are straight line segments.
    a. Triangle0
    b. Thing
    c. Undefined
    d. Undefined

77. In geometry, a _____ is a special kind of point, usually a corner of a polygon, polyhedron, or higher dimensional polytope. In the geometry of curves a _____ is a point of where the first derivative of curvature is zero. In graph theory, a _____ is the fundamental unit out of which graphs are formed

Chapter 4. Linear Transformations

    a. Thing   b. Vertex0
    c. Undefined   d. Undefined

78. The _____ of an angle is the ratio of the length of the adjacent side to the length of the hypotenuse.
    a. Concept   b. Cosine0
    c. Undefined   d. Undefined

79. The _____ is a statement about a general triangle which relates the lengths of its sides to the cosine of one of its angles.
    a. Thing   b. Law of cosines0
    c. Undefined   d. Undefined

80. _____ in a normed vector space is a vector whose length, or magnitude is 1.
    a. Thing   b. Unit vector0
    c. Undefined   d. Undefined

81. In linear algebra, two vectors in an inner product space are _____ if they are orthogonal (their inner product is 0) and both of unit length (the norm of each is 1). A set of vectors which is pairwise _____ (any two vectors in it are _____) is called an _____ set. A basis which forms an _____ set is called an _____ basis.
    a. Orthonormal0   b. Thing
    c. Undefined   d. Undefined

82. In mathematics, suppose C is a collection of mathematical objects . Then we say that C is _____ if every c ∊ C is uniquely determined by less information about c than one would expect.
    a. Thing   b. Rigid0
    c. Undefined   d. Undefined

83. In Euclidean mathematics, _____ consists of a transformation of the plane or space, which preserves distance and angles.
    a. Rigid motion0   b. Thing
    c. Undefined   d. Undefined

84. In Euclidean geometry, a _____ is moving every point a constant distance in a specified direction.
    a. Concept   b. Translation0
    c. Undefined   d. Undefined

85. In mathematics, an _____ on a real vector space is a choice of which ordered bases are "positively" oriented, or right-handed, and which are "negatively" oriented, or left-handed.
    a. Thing   b. Orientation0
    c. Undefined   d. Undefined

86. Mathematical _____ is used to represent ideas.
    a. Notation0   b. Thing
    c. Undefined   d. Undefined

Chapter 4. Linear Transformations

87. In mathematics, a _____ number (or a _____) is a natural number that has exactly two (distinct) natural number divisors, which are 1 and the _____ number itself.
    a. Prime0
    b. Thing
    c. Undefined
    d. Undefined

88. _____ also called natural basis or canonical basis of the n-dimensional Euclidean space Rn is the basis obtained by taking the n basis vectors
    a. Standard basis0
    b. Thing
    c. Undefined
    d. Undefined

89. In mathematics, factorization (British English: factorisation) or factoring is the decomposition of an object (for example, a number, a polynomial, or a matrix) into a product of other objects, or _____, which when multiplied together give the original.
    a. Thing
    b. Factors0
    c. Undefined
    d. Undefined

90. A _____ is traditionally an infinitesimally small change in a variable.
    a. Thing
    b. Differential0
    c. Undefined
    d. Undefined

91. A _____ is a mathematical equation for an unknown function of one or several variables which relates the values of the function itself and of its derivatives of various orders.
    a. Differential equation0
    b. Thing
    c. Undefined
    d. Undefined

92. _____ is a mathematical subject that includes the study of limits, derivatives, integrals, and power series and constitutes a major part of modern university curriculum.
    a. Calculus0
    b. Thing
    c. Undefined
    d. Undefined

93. The mathematical concept of a _____ expresses the intuitive idea of deterministic dependence between two quantities, one of which is viewed as primary and the other as secondary. A _____ then is a way to associate a unique output for each input of a specified type, for example, a real number or an element of a given set.
    a. Thing
    b. Function0
    c. Undefined
    d. Undefined

94. In mathematics and the mathematical sciences, a _____ is a fixed, but possibly unspecified, value. This is in contrast to a variable, which is not fixed.
    a. Constant0
    b. Thing
    c. Undefined
    d. Undefined

95. _____, a field in mathematics, is the study of how functions change when their inputs change. The primary object of study in _____ is the derivative.
    a. Differential calculus0
    b. Thing
    c. Undefined
    d. Undefined

Chapter 4. Linear Transformations

96. In combinatorial mathematics, a _____ is an un-ordered collection of unique elements.
    a. Concept
    b. Combination0
    c. Undefined
    d. Undefined

97. The _____ governs the differentiation of products of differentiable functions.
    a. Thing
    b. Product rule0
    c. Undefined
    d. Undefined

98. In mathematics, an _____ number is a complex number whose square is a negative real number. They were defined in 1572 by Rafael Bombelli.
    a. Imaginary0
    b. Thing
    c. Undefined
    d. Undefined

99. In mathematics, the _____ of a complex number z, is the second element of the ordered pair of real numbers representing z, i.e. if z = (x,y), or equivalently, z = x + iy, then the _____ of z is y.
    a. Thing
    b. Imaginary part0
    c. Undefined
    d. Undefined

100. In mathematics, _____ growth occurs when the growth rate of a function is always proportional to the function's current size.
    a. Thing
    b. Exponential0
    c. Undefined
    d. Undefined

101. A _____ is the sum of the elements of a sequence.
    a. Thing
    b. Series0
    c. Undefined
    d. Undefined

102. Two mathematical objects are equal if and only if they are precisely the same in every way. This defines a binary relation, _____, denoted by the sign of _____ "=" in such a way that the statement "x = y" means that x and y are equal.
    a. Thing
    b. Equality0
    c. Undefined
    d. Undefined

103. The _____ is a rule which states that when you add or multiply numbers, changing the order doesn't change the result.
    a. Commutative law0
    b. Thing
    c. Undefined
    d. Undefined

104. An _____ of a product of sums expresses it as a sum of products by using the fact that multiplication distributes over addition.
    a. Thing
    b. Expansion0
    c. Undefined
    d. Undefined

105. In mathematics and logic, a _____ proof is a way of showing the truth or falsehood of a given statement by a straightforward combination of established facts, usually existing lemmas and theorems, without making any further assumptions.

Chapter 4. Linear Transformations

a. Direct0
b. Thing
c. Undefined
d. Undefined

106. In mathematics, _____ describes an entity with a limit.
a. Thing
b. Convergent0
c. Undefined
d. Undefined

107. In mathematics, the _____ (or modulus) of a real number is its numerical value without regard to its sign.
a. Absolute value0
b. Thing
c. Undefined
d. Undefined

108. _____ was a British mathematician. He helped found the modern British school of pure mathematics.
a. Person
b. Arthur Cayley0
c. Undefined
d. Undefined

109. _____ is an operator defined as a function of the _____.
a. Thing
b. Differentiation operator0
c. Undefined
d. Undefined

110. In linear algebra, a _____ is a 1 × n matrix, that is, a matrix consisting of a single row
a. Thing
b. Row vector0
c. Undefined
d. Undefined

111. In mathematics, an element x of a ring R is called _____ if there exists some positive integer n such that $x^n = 0$.
a. Nilpotent0
b. Thing
c. Undefined
d. Undefined

112. A _____ of a number is the product of that number with any integer.
a. Multiple0
b. Thing
c. Undefined
d. Undefined

113. In mathematics, a _____ (also spelled reflexion) is a map that transforms an object into its mirror image.
a. Reflection0
b. Concept
c. Undefined
d. Undefined

114. _____ is a circle with a unit radius, i.e., a circle whose radius is 1.
a. Unit circle0
b. Thing
c. Undefined
d. Undefined

115. In Euclidean geometry, a _____ is the set of all points in a plane at a fixed distance, called the radius, from a given point, the center.
a. Circle0
b. Thing
c. Undefined
d. Undefined

Chapter 4. Linear Transformations

116. In linear algebra, a square matrix A is called _____ if it is similar to a diagonal matrix, i.e. if there exists an invertible matrix P such that P −1AP is a diagonal matrix. If V is a finite-dimensional vector space, then a linear map T : V → V is called _____ if there exists a basis of V with respect to which T is represented by a diagonal matrix. Diagonalization is the process of finding a corresponding diagonal matrix for a _____ matrix or linear map.
   a. Diagonalizable0
   b. Thing
   c. Undefined
   d. Undefined

117. In mathematics, a _____ is an ordered list of objects. Like a set, it contains members, also called elements or terms, and the number of terms is called the length of the _____. Unlike a set, order matters, and the exact same elements can appear multiple times at different positions in the _____.
   a. Sequence0
   b. Thing
   c. Undefined
   d. Undefined

118. A _____ function is a function for which, intuitively, small changes in the input result in small changes in the output.
   a. Event
   b. Continuous0
   c. Undefined
   d. Undefined

119. In elementary algebra, an _____ is a set that contains every real number between two indicated numbers and may contain the two numbers themselves.
   a. Interval0
   b. Thing
   c. Undefined
   d. Undefined

120. In linear algebra, a _____ is a square matrix, A, that is equal to its transpose.
   a. Thing
   b. Symmetric Matrix0
   c. Undefined
   d. Undefined

121. In calculus, the _____ is a formula for the derivative of the composite of two functions.
   a. Concept
   b. Chain rule0
   c. Undefined
   d. Undefined

122. _____ in one variable is an infinite series of the form
   a. Power series0
   b. Thing
   c. Undefined
   d. Undefined

123. In linear algebra, a _____ of a matrix A is the determinant of some smaller square matrix, cut down from A.
   a. Thing
   b. Minor0
   c. Undefined
   d. Undefined

124. _____ element of an element x with respect to a binary operation * with identity element e is an element y such that x * y = y * x = e. In particular,
   a. Thing
   b. Inverse0
   c. Undefined
   d. Undefined

125. An _____ is a combination of numbers, operators, grouping symbols and/or free variables and bound variables arranged in a meaningful way which can be evaluated..

a. Expression0 b. Thing
c. Undefined d. Undefined

126. The _____ integers are all the integers from zero on upwards.
a. Thing b. Nonnegative0
c. Undefined d. Undefined

Chapter 5. Symmetry

1. _____ is that branch of mathematics concerned with the study of groups. These are sets with a rule, or operation. The operation in a group must satisfy closure and have these three additional properties: 1) The operation must have the property of associativity. 2) There must be an identity element. 3) Every element must have a corresponding inverse element. _____ is used throughout mathematics and has several applications in physics and chemistry. Groups can be finite or infinite. A classification of finite simple groups, completed in 1983, is one of the major achievements of mathematics in the 20th century.
   a. Group theory0
   b. Thing
   c. Undefined
   d. Undefined

2. Marie-_____ (April 1, 1776 – June 27, 1831) was an important French mathematician.
   a. Sophie Germain0
   b. Person
   c. Undefined
   d. Undefined

3. _____ means "constancy", i.e. if something retains a certain feature even after we change a way of looking at it, then it is symmetric.
   a. Symmetry0
   b. Thing
   c. Undefined
   d. Undefined

4. In mathematics, more specifically in abstract algebra, a _____ is the main object of study in field theory. The general idea is to start with a base field and construct in some manner a larger field which contains the base field and satisfies additional properties.
   a. Field extension0
   b. Thing
   c. Undefined
   d. Undefined

5. In group theory, given a group G under a binary operation *, we say that some subset H of G is a _____ of G if H also forms a group under the operation *.
   a. Thing
   b. Subgroup0
   c. Undefined
   d. Undefined

6. A _____ is a set whose members are members of another set or a set contained within another set.
   a. Subset0
   b. Thing
   c. Undefined
   d. Undefined

7. In mathematics, suppose C is a collection of mathematical objects . Then we say that C is _____ if every c ∈ C is uniquely determined by less information about c than one would expect.
   a. Rigid0
   b. Thing
   c. Undefined
   d. Undefined

8. In mathematics, a _____ is a two-dimensional manifold or surface that is perfectly flat.
   a. Thing
   b. Plane0
   c. Undefined
   d. Undefined

9. In mathematics, a _____ in elementary terms is any of a variety of different functions from geometry, such as rotations, reflections and translations.
   a. Thing
   b. Transformation0
   c. Undefined
   d. Undefined

10. An _____ or member of a set is an object that when collected together make up the set.
   a. Element0
   b. Thing
   c. Undefined
   d. Undefined

11. In mathematics, the _____ , or members of a set or more generally a class are all those objects which when collected together make up the set or class.
   a. Thing
   b. Elements0
   c. Undefined
   d. Undefined

12. In mathematics, a _____ (also spelled reflexion) is a map that transforms an object into its mirror image.
   a. Reflection0
   b. Concept
   c. Undefined
   d. Undefined

13. An _____ is a straight line around which a geometric figure can be rotated.
   a. Thing
   b. Axis0
   c. Undefined
   d. Undefined

14. _____ of a two-dimensional figure is a line such that, if a perpendicular is constructed, any two points lying on the perpendicular at equal distances from the _____ are identical.
   a. Thing
   b. Axis of symmetry0
   c. Undefined
   d. Undefined

15. An _____ is an equality that remains true regardless of the values of any variables that appear within it, to distinguish it from an equality which is true under more particular conditions.
   a. Thing
   b. Identity0
   c. Undefined
   d. Undefined

16. In mathematics, an identity function, also called identity map or _____, is a function that does not have any effect: it always returns the same value that was used as its argument. In other words, the identity function is the function f = x.
   a. Thing
   b. Identity transformation0
   c. Undefined
   d. Undefined

17. In Euclidean geometry, a _____ is moving every point a constant distance in a specified direction.
   a. Translation0
   b. Concept
   c. Undefined
   d. Undefined

18. In physics and in _____ calculus, a spatial _____, or simply _____, is a concept characterized by a magnitude and a direction.
   a. Thing
   b. Vector0
   c. Undefined
   d. Undefined

19. Statistical _____ is a statistical procedure in which individual items are placed into groups based on quantitative information on one or more characteristics inherent in the items and based on a training set of previously labeled items.
   a. Classification0
   b. Thing
   c. Undefined
   d. Undefined

Chapter 5. Symmetry

20. In mathematics, an _____ on a real vector space is a choice of which ordered bases are "positively" oriented, or right-handed, and which are "negatively" oriented, or left-handed.
    a. Thing
    b. Orientation0
    c. Undefined
    d. Undefined

21. A _____ is a movement of an object in a circular motion. A two-dimensional object rotates around a center (or point) of _____. A three-dimensional object rotates around a line called an axis. If the axis of _____ is within the body, the body is said to rotate upon itself, or spin—which implies relative speed and perhaps free-movement with angular momentum. A circular motion about an external point, e.g. the Earth about the Sun, is called an orbit or more properly an orbital revolution.
    a. Thing
    b. Rotation0
    c. Undefined
    d. Undefined

22. A _____ ratio, also called, Lift-to-drag ratio, _____ number, or finesse, is an aviation term that refers to the distance an aircraft will move forward for any given amount of lost altitude .
    a. Thing
    b. Glide0
    c. Undefined
    d. Undefined

23. In geometry, a _____ is a type of isometry of the Euclidean plane: the combination of a reflection in a line and a translation along that line.
    a. Thing
    b. Glide reflection0
    c. Undefined
    d. Undefined

24. In Euclidean mathematics, _____ consists of a transformation of the plane or space, which preserves distance and angles.
    a. Rigid motion0
    b. Thing
    c. Undefined
    d. Undefined

25. In mathematics, a _____ of a positive integer n is a way of writing n as a sum of positive integers.
    a. Thing
    b. Composition0
    c. Undefined
    d. Undefined

26. A _____ is the result of the addition of a set of numbers. The numbers may be natural numbers, complex numbers, matrices, or still more complicated objects. An infinite _____ is a subtle procedure known as a series.
    a. Thing
    b. Sum0
    c. Undefined
    d. Undefined

27. In mathematics, _____ is synonymous with perpendicular when used as a simple adjective that is not part of any longer phrase with a standard definition. It means at right angles. It comes from the Greek ἀ½€ἰ ἰ¸ἰŒἰ, orthos, meaning "straight", used by Euclid to mean right; and ἰᵃἰ‰ἰ½ἰ¯ ἰ± gonia, meaning angle. Two streets that cross each other at a right angle are _____ to one another.
    a. Orthogonal0
    b. Thing
    c. Undefined
    d. Undefined

28. The existence and properties of _____ are the basis of Euclid's parallel postulate. _____ are two lines on the same plane that do not intersect even assuming that lines extend to infinity in either direction.

Chapter 5. Symmetry

a. Parallel lines0
b. Thing
c. Undefined
d. Undefined

29. The _____ functions is determined by the nesting of two or more functions to form a single new function.
a. Composition of two0
b. Thing
c. Undefined
d. Undefined

30. In mathematics, a _____ is a statement that can be proved on the basis of explicitly stated or previously agreed assumptions.
a. Thing
b. Theorem0
c. Undefined
d. Undefined

31. In mathematics, the _____ of a coordinate system is the point where the axes of the system intersect.
a. Thing
b. Origin0
c. Undefined
d. Undefined

32. In linear algebra and related areas of mathematics, the null vector or _____ is the vector in Euclidean space, all of whose components are zero.
a. Zero vector0
b. Thing
c. Undefined
d. Undefined

33. The word _____ comes from the Latin word linearis, which means created by lines.
a. Linear0
b. Thing
c. Undefined
d. Undefined

34. In mathematics, a _____ is the result of multiplying, or an expression that identifies factors to be multiplied.
a. Product0
b. Thing
c. Undefined
d. Undefined

35. An _____ is a combination of numbers, operators, grouping symbols and/or free variables and bound variables arranged in a meaningful way which can be evaluated..
a. Expression0
b. Thing
c. Undefined
d. Undefined

36. In mathematics, a _____ is a demonstration that, assuming certain axioms, some statement is necessarily true.
a. Thing
b. Proof0
c. Undefined
d. Undefined

37. A circular _____ or circle _____ also known as a pie piece is the portion of a circle enclosed by two radii and an arc.
a. Thing
b. Sector0
c. Undefined
d. Undefined

38. In geometry, two lines or planes if one falls on the other in such a way as to create congruent adjacent angles. The term may be used as a noun or adjective. Thus, referring to Figure 1, the line AB is the _____ to CD through the point B.

Chapter 5. Symmetry

a. Perpendicular0
b. Thing
c. Undefined
d. Undefined

39. A _____ is a negotiable instrument instructing a financial institution to pay a specific amount of a specific currency from a specific demand account held in the maker/depositor's name with that institution. Both the maker and payee may be natural persons or legal entities.
a. Thing
b. Check0
c. Undefined
d. Undefined

40. A _____ is a set of numbers that designate location in a given reference system, such as x,y in a planar _____ system or an x,y,z in a three-dimensional _____ system.
a. Coordinate0
b. Thing
c. Undefined
d. Undefined

41. In mathematics, a _____ is a rectangular table of numbers or, more generally, a table consisting of abstract quantities that can be added and multiplied.
a. Matrix0
b. Thing
c. Undefined
d. Undefined

42. In mathematics, an _____ (Greek:isos "equal", and morphe "shape") is a bijective map f such that both f and its inverse f^{-1} are homomorphisms, i.e. *structure-preserving* mappings.
a. Isomorphism0
b. Thing
c. Undefined
d. Undefined

43. In category theory and its applications to other branches of mathematics, _____ are a generalization of the kernels of group homomorphisms and the kernels of module homomorphisms and certain other kernels from algebra.
a. Thing
b. Kernel0
c. Undefined
d. Undefined

44. In abstract algebra, a _____ is a structure-preserving map between two algebraic structures. The word _____ comes from the Greek language: homo meaning "same" and morphi meaning "shape".
a. Homomorphism0
b. Thing
c. Undefined
d. Undefined

45. _____ is the state of being greater than any finite real or natural number, however large.
a. Infinite0
b. Thing
c. Undefined
d. Undefined

46. In mathematics, a set is called _____ if there is a bijection between the set and some set of the form {1, 2, ..., n} where n is a natural number.
a. Finite0
b. Thing
c. Undefined
d. Undefined

47. In mathematics, a _____ is a result saying that a function F will have at least one fixed point , under some conditions on F that can be stated in general terms.

Chapter 5. Symmetry

a. Thing
b. Fixed point theorem0
c. Undefined
d. Undefined

48. In mathematics, a _____ function in the sense of algebraic geometry is an everywhere-defined, polynomial function on an algebraic variety V with values in the field K over which V is defined.
a. Thing
b. Regular0
c. Undefined
d. Undefined

49. In physics, an _____ is the path that an object makes around another object while under the influence of a source of centripetal force, such as gravity.
a. Thing
b. Orbit0
c. Undefined
d. Undefined

50. In mathematics, an _____ (or neutral element) is a special type of element of a set with respect to a binary operation on that set.
a. Identity element0
b. Concept
c. Undefined
d. Undefined

51. In mathematics, _____ is a part of the set theoretic notion of function.
a. Thing
b. Image0
c. Undefined
d. Undefined

52. In geometry, a _____ is any five-sided polygon.
a. Pentagon0
b. Thing
c. Undefined
d. Undefined

53. In geometry, the _____ of an object is a point in some sense in the middle of the object.
a. Thing
b. Center0
c. Undefined
d. Undefined

54. In mathematics and its applications, a _____ is a system for assigning an n-tuple of numbers or scalars to each point in an n-dimensional space.
a. Coordinate system0
b. Concept
c. Undefined
d. Undefined

55. In mathematics, an _____, mean, or central tendency of a data set refers to a measure of the "middle" or "expected" value of the data set.
a. Concept
b. Average0
c. Undefined
d. Undefined

56. In mathematics, a _____ occurs if there is a bijection between the set and some set of the form 1, 2, ..., n where n is a natural number.
a. Concept
b. Finite set0
c. Undefined
d. Undefined

Chapter 5. Symmetry

57. In mathematics, the _____ of order 2n is the abstract group of which one representation is the symmetry group in 2D of a regular polygon with n sides
   a. Thing
   b. Dihedral group0
   c. Undefined
   d. Undefined

58. In geometry a _____ is a plane figure that is bounded by a closed path or circuit, composed of a finite number of sequential line segments.
   a. Thing
   b. Polygon0
   c. Undefined
   d. Undefined

59. _____ has many meanings, most of which simply .
   a. Power0
   b. Thing
   c. Undefined
   d. Undefined

60. Equivalence is the condition of being _____ or essentially equal.
   a. Equivalent0
   b. Thing
   c. Undefined
   d. Undefined

61. The _____ are the only integral domain whose positive elements are well-ordered, and in which order is preserved by addition. Like the natural numbers, the _____ form a countably infinite set. The set of all _____ is usually denoted in mathematics by a boldface Z .
   a. Integers0
   b. Thing
   c. Undefined
   d. Undefined

62. In mathematics, the _____ inverse, or opposite, of a number n is the number that, when added to n, yields zero. The _____ inverse of n is denoted −n.
   a. Thing
   b. Additive0
   c. Undefined
   d. Undefined

63. In group theory, a _____ or monogenous group is a group that can be generated by a single element, in the sense that the group has an element g called a "generator" of the group such that, when written multiplicatively, every element of the group is a power of g a multiple of g when the notation is additive.
   a. Thing
   b. Cyclic group0
   c. Undefined
   d. Undefined

64. In Euclidean geometry, a _____ is the set of all points in a plane at a fixed distance, called the radius, from a given point, the center.
   a. Thing
   b. Circle0
   c. Undefined
   d. Undefined

65. In linear algebra and geometry, a rotation (_____) is a type of transformation from one system of coordinates to another system of coordinates such that distance between any two points remains invariant under the transformation.
   a. Rotational0
   b. Thing
   c. Undefined
   d. Undefined

66. A _____ is 360° or 2δ radians.

Chapter 5. Symmetry

a. Turn0
b. Thing
c. Undefined
d. Undefined

67. The word _____ comes from the 15th Century Latin word discretus which means separate.
    a. Thing
    b. Discrete0
    c. Undefined
    d. Undefined

68. A _____ signifies a point or points of probability on a subject e.g., the _____ of creativity, which allows for the formation of rule or norm or law by interpretation of the phenomena events that can be created.
    a. Principle0
    b. Thing
    c. Undefined
    d. Undefined

69. A _____ (or shape) refers to the external two-dimensional outline, appearance or configuration of some thing - in contrast to the matter or content or substance of which it is composed.
    a. Plane figure0
    b. Thing
    c. Undefined
    d. Undefined

70. _____ is a set, with some particular properties and usually some additional structure, such as the operations of addition or multiplication, for instance.
    a. Space0
    b. Thing
    c. Undefined
    d. Undefined

71. The _____, the average in everyday English, which is also called the arithmetic _____ (and is distinguished from the geometric _____ or harmonic _____). The average is also called the sample _____. The expected value of a random variable, which is also called the population _____.
    a. Thing
    b. Mean0
    c. Undefined
    d. Undefined

72. In mathematics, a _____ is a partially ordered set (or poset) in which every pair of elements has a unique supremum (the elements' least upper bound; called their join) and an infimum (greatest lower bound; called their meet).
    a. Lattice0
    b. Concept
    c. Undefined
    d. Undefined

73. In mathematical analysis and related areas of mathematics, a set is called _____, if it is, in a certain sense, of finite size.
    a. Thing
    b. Bounded0
    c. Undefined
    d. Undefined

74. In mathematical analysis and related areas of mathematics, a set is called a _____, if it is, in a certain sense, of finite size.
    a. Thing
    b. Bounded set0
    c. Undefined
    d. Undefined

75. In classical geometry, a _____ of a circle or sphere is any line segment from its center to its boundary. By extension, the _____ of a circle or sphere is the length of any such segment. The _____ is half the diameter. In science and engineering the term _____ of curvature is commonly used as a synonym for _____.

a. Thing
b. Radius0
c. Undefined
d. Undefined

76. A _____ of a number is the product of that number with any integer.
    a. Thing
    b. Multiple0
    c. Undefined
    d. Undefined

77. A _____ is a four-sided plane figure that has two sets of opposite parallel sides.
    a. Parallelogram0
    b. Concept
    c. Undefined
    d. Undefined

78. In geometry, a line _____ is a part of a line that is bounded by two end points, and contains every point on the line between its end points.
    a. Concept
    b. Segment0
    c. Undefined
    d. Undefined

79. In geometry, a _____ is a special kind of point, usually a corner of a polygon, polyhedron, or higher dimensional polytope. In the geometry of curves a _____ is a point of where the first derivative of curvature is zero. In graph theory, a _____ is the fundamental unit out of which graphs are formed
    a. Vertex0
    b. Thing
    c. Undefined
    d. Undefined

80. A _____ is a part of a line that is bounded by two end points, and contains every point on the line between its end points.
    a. Line segment0
    b. Thing
    c. Undefined
    d. Undefined

81. In mathematics, a _____ may be described informally as a number that can be given by an infinite decimal representation.
    a. Real number0
    b. Thing
    c. Undefined
    d. Undefined

82. In combinatorial mathematics, a _____ is an un-ordered collection of unique elements.
    a. Combination0
    b. Concept
    c. Undefined
    d. Undefined

83. _____ the expected value of a random variable displays the average or central value of the variable. It is a summary value of the distribution of the variable.
    a. Thing
    b. Determining0
    c. Undefined
    d. Undefined

84. _____ is a subset of a population.
    a. Sample0
    b. Thing
    c. Undefined
    d. Undefined

Chapter 5. Symmetry

85. Deductive _____ is the kind of _____ in which the conclusion is necessitated by, or reached from, previously known facts (the premises).
    a. Reasoning0
    b. Thing
    c. Undefined
    d. Undefined

86. In plane geometry, a _____ is a polygon with four equal sides, four right angles, and parallel opposite sides. In algebra, the _____ of a number is that number multiplied by itself.
    a. Square0
    b. Thing
    c. Undefined
    d. Undefined

87. In mathematics, _____ is an elementary arithmetic operation. When one of the numbers is a whole number, _____ is the repeated sum of the other number.
    a. Thing
    b. Multiplication0
    c. Undefined
    d. Undefined

88. In common philosophical language, a proposition or _____, is the content of an assertion, that is, it is true-or-false and defined by the meaning of a particular piece of language.
    a. Concept
    b. Statement0
    c. Undefined
    d. Undefined

89. In mathematics, an _____ is an isomorphism from a mathematical objct of itself while preserving all of its structure.
    a. Thing
    b. Automorphism0
    c. Undefined
    d. Undefined

90. In algebra, a _____ is a binomial formed by taking the opposite of the second term of a binomial.
    a. Conjugate0
    b. Thing
    c. Undefined
    d. Undefined

91. A _____, is a symbolized depiction of space which highlights relations between components of that space. Most usually a _____ is a two-dimensional, geometrically accurate representation of a three-dimensional space.
    a. Thing
    b. Map0
    c. Undefined
    d. Undefined

92. In mathematics, a _____ is a number in the form of a + bi where a and b are real numbers, and i is the imaginary unit, with the property i 2 = −1. The real number a is called the real part of the _____, and the real number b is the imaginary part.
    a. Complex number0
    b. Thing
    c. Undefined
    d. Undefined

93. An _____ is any starting assumption from which other statements are logically derived
    a. Axiom0
    b. Thing
    c. Undefined
    d. Undefined

94. In mathematics, if G is a group, H a subgroup of G, and g an element of G, then, gH = {gh : h an element of H } is a left _____ of H in G, and Hg = {hg : h an element of H } is a right _____ of H in G.

a. Coset0
b. Thing
c. Undefined
d. Undefined

95. Mathematical _____ is used to represent ideas.
   a. Notation0
   b. Thing
   c. Undefined
   d. Undefined

96. _____ is bother the congnitive process of transferring information from a particular subject , and a linguistic expression corresponding to such a process.
   a. Analogy0
   b. Thing
   c. Undefined
   d. Undefined

97. A _____ is one of the basic shapes of geometry: a polygon with three vertices and three sides which are straight line segments.
   a. Triangle0
   b. Thing
   c. Undefined
   d. Undefined

98. In set theory and other branches of mathematics, the _____ of a collection of sets is the set that contains everything that belongs to any of the sets, but nothing else.
   a. Union0
   b. Thing
   c. Undefined
   d. Undefined

99. In set theory and its applications throughout mathematics, _____ are a collection of sets (or sometimes other mathematical objects) that can be unambiguously defined by a property that all its members share.
   a. Thing
   b. Classes0
   c. Undefined
   d. Undefined

100. An _____ is a binary relation between two elements of a set which groups them together as being equivalent in some way.
   a. Equivalence relation0
   b. Thing
   c. Undefined
   d. Undefined

101. Generally, a _____ is a splitting of something into parts.
   a. Partition0
   b. Thing
   c. Undefined
   d. Undefined

102. _____ is the rearrangement of objects or symbols into distinguishable sequences.
   a. Permutation0
   b. Thing
   c. Undefined
   d. Undefined

103. In geometry, two sets are called _____ if one can be transformed into the other by an isometry, i.e., a combination of translations, rotations and reflections.
   a. Congruent0
   b. Thing
   c. Undefined
   d. Undefined

Chapter 5. Symmetry

104. In mathematics, two sets are said to be _____ if they have no element in common. For example, {1, 2, 3} and {4, 5, 6} are sets which are _____.
   a. Disjoint0
   b. Thing
   c. Undefined
   d. Undefined

105. In geometry, an _____ polygon is a polygon which has all sides of the same length.
   a. Thing
   b. Equilateral0
   c. Undefined
   d. Undefined

106. An _____ is a triangle in which all sides are of equal length.
   a. Thing
   b. Equilateral triangle0
   c. Undefined
   d. Undefined

107. _____ are objects, characters, or other concrete representations of ideas, concepts, or other abstractions.
   a. Symbols0
   b. Thing
   c. Undefined
   d. Undefined

108. Mathematical _____ are the wide variety of ways to capture an abstract mathematical concept or relationship.
   a. Thing
   b. Representations0
   c. Undefined
   d. Undefined

109. In mathematics, a _____ is a constant multiplicative factor of a certain object. The object can be such things as a variable, a vector, a function, etc. For example, the _____ of $9x^2$ is 9.
   a. Thing
   b. Coefficient0
   c. Undefined
   d. Undefined

110. In mathematics, the idea of _____ generalises the concepts of negation, in relation to addition, and reciprocal, in relation to multiplication.
   a. Inverse element0
   b. Thing
   c. Undefined
   d. Undefined

111. In mathematics, the _____ inverse of a number x, denoted 1/x or x^{-1}, is the number which, when multiplied by x, yields 1. The _____ inverse of x is also called the reciprocal of x.
   a. Thing
   b. Multiplicative0
   c. Undefined
   d. Undefined

112. In mathematics, a _____ is the set of all points in three-dimensional space (R^3) which are at distance r from a fixed point of that space, where r is a positive real number called the radius of the _____. The fixed point is called the center or centre, and is not part of the _____ itself.
   a. Sphere0
   b. Thing
   c. Undefined
   d. Undefined

113. _____ is the mathematical action of repeatedly adding or subtracting one, usually to find out how many objects there are or to set aside a desired number of objects.

a. Thing
b. Counting0
c. Undefined
d. Undefined

114. The plus and _____ signs are mathematical symbols used to represent the notions of positive and negative as well as the operations of addition and subtraction.
a. Minus0
b. Thing
c. Undefined
d. Undefined

115. A _____ is a three-dimensional solid object bounded by six square faces, facets, or sides, with three meeting at each vertex.
a. Cube0
b. Thing
c. Undefined
d. Undefined

116. An _____ is a polyhedron with eight faces.
a. Octahedron0
b. Thing
c. Undefined
d. Undefined

117. A _____ (plural: tetrahedra) is a polyhedron composed of four triangular faces, three of which meet at each vertex.
a. Tetrahedron0
b. Thing
c. Undefined
d. Undefined

118. An icosahedronis any polyhedron having 20 faces, but usually a regular _____ is implied, which has equilateral triangles as faces.
a. Icosahedron0
b. Thing
c. Undefined
d. Undefined

119. A _____ (plural polyhedra or polyhedrons) is a geometric object with flat faces and straight edges.
a. Polyhedron0
b. Thing
c. Undefined
d. Undefined

120. A _____ is any polyhedron with twelve faces, but usually a regular _____ is meant: a Platonic solid composed of twelve regular pentagonal faces, with three meeting at each vertex.
a. Thing
b. Dodecahedron0
c. Undefined
d. Undefined

121. A _____ is a deliberate process for transforming one or more inputs into one or more results.
a. Calculation0
b. Thing
c. Undefined
d. Undefined

122. A vector can be thought of as an arrow. It has a length, called its magnitude, and it points in some particular direction. A linear transformation inputs a vector and changes it, usually changing both its magnitude and its direction. An eigenvector of a given linear transformation is a vector which is simply multiplied by a constant called the _____ during that transformation.

Chapter 5. Symmetry

a. Eigenvalue0   b. Thing
c. Undefined   d. Undefined

123. An _____ of a linear transformation is a non-zero vector that is either left unaffected or simply multiplied by a scale factor after the transformation.
   a. Eigenvector0
   b. Thing
   c. Undefined
   d. Undefined

124. The word _____ is used in a variety of ways in mathematics.
   a. Thing
   b. Index0
   c. Undefined
   d. Undefined

125. An _____ is when two lines intersect somewhere on a plane creating a right angle at intersection
   a. Thing
   b. Axes0
   c. Undefined
   d. Undefined

126. A _____ is a symbolic representation denoting a quantity or expression. It often represents an "unknown" quantity that has the potential to change.
   a. Thing
   b. Variable0
   c. Undefined
   d. Undefined

127. A _____ fraction is a fraction in which the absolute value of the numerator is less than the denominator--hence, the absolute value of the fraction is less than 1.
   a. Proper0
   b. Thing
   c. Undefined
   d. Undefined

128. In mathematics, a _____ is the end result of a division problem. It can also be expressed as the number of times the divisor divides into the dividend.
   a. Thing
   b. Quotient0
   c. Undefined
   d. Undefined

129. A _____ is a mathematical statement which follows easily from a previously proven statement, typically a mathematical theorem.
   a. Thing
   b. Corollary0
   c. Undefined
   d. Undefined

130. In mathematics and logic, a _____ proof is a way of showing the truth or falsehood of a given statement by a straightforward combination of established facts, usually existing lemmas and theorems, without making any further assumptions.
   a. Thing
   b. Direct0
   c. Undefined
   d. Undefined

131. A frame of _____ is a particular perspective from which the universe is observed.
   a. Reference0
   b. Thing
   c. Undefined
   d. Undefined

Chapter 5. Symmetry

132. In mathematics, a _____ case is a limiting case in which a class of object changes its nature so as to belong to another, usually simpler, class.
   a. Thing
   b. Degenerate0
   c. Undefined
   d. Undefined

133. In physics, the _____ momentum of an object rotating about some reference point is the measure of the extent to which the object will continue to rotate about that point unless acted upon by an external torque.
   a. Angular0
   b. Thing
   c. Undefined
   d. Undefined

134. A _____ can refer to a line joining two nonadjacent vertices of a polygon or polyhedron, or in some contexts any upward or downward sloping line. .
   a. Diagonal0
   b. Thing
   c. Undefined
   d. Undefined

135. _____ refers to the reduction of the body of a formerly living organism into simpler forms of matter.
   a. Decomposing0
   b. Thing
   c. Undefined
   d. Undefined

136. In mathematics, a _____ number is a number which can be expressed as a ratio of two integers. Non-integer _____ numbers (commonly called fractions) are usually written as the vulgar fraction a / b, where b is not zero.
   a. Thing
   b. Rational0
   c. Undefined
   d. Undefined

137. In mathematics, _____ are two-dimensional manifolds or surfaces that are perfectly flat.
   a. Thing
   b. Planes0
   c. Undefined
   d. Undefined

138. In mathematics, the _____ of two sets A and B is the set that contains all elements of A that also belong to B (or equivalently, all elements of B that also belong to A), but no other elements.
   a. Intersection0
   b. Thing
   c. Undefined
   d. Undefined

139. In mathematics, a matrix can be thought of as each row or _____ being a vector. Hence, a space formed by row vectors or _____ vectors are said to be a row space or a _____ space.
   a. Column0
   b. Concept
   c. Undefined
   d. Undefined

140. _____ is an m × 1 matrix, i.e. a matrix consisting of a single column of m elements.
   a. Thing
   b. Column vector0
   c. Undefined
   d. Undefined

141. An _____ is a square matrix which has an inverse.
   a. Thing
   b. Invertible matrix0
   c. Undefined
   d. Undefined

Chapter 5. Symmetry

142. In mathematics, the additive inverse, or _____ of a number n is the number that, when added to n, yields zero. The additive inverse of n is denoted −n. For example, 7 is −7, because 7 + (−7) = 0, and the additive inverse of −0.3 is 0.3, because −0.3 + 0.3 = 0.
   a. Thing
   b. Opposite0
   c. Undefined
   d. Undefined

143. In mathematics, the _____ of a number n is the number that, when added to n, yields zero. The _____ of n is denoted −n. For example, 7 is −7, because 7 + (−7) = 0, and the _____ of −0.3 is 0.3, because −0.3 + 0.3 = 0.
   a. Thing
   b. Additive inverse0
   c. Undefined
   d. Undefined

144. In mathematics, the concept of a _____ tries to capture the intuitive idea of a geometrical one-dimensional and continuous object. A simple example is the circle.
   a. Curve0
   b. Thing
   c. Undefined
   d. Undefined

145. In mathematics, _____ are the intuitive idea of a geometrical one-dimensional and continuous object.
   a. Thing
   b. Curves0
   c. Undefined
   d. Undefined

146. A _____ defined function f(x) of a real variable x is a function whose definition is given differently on disjoint subsets of its domain.
   a. Piecewise0
   b. Thing
   c. Undefined
   d. Undefined

147. In mathematics, a _____ of a k-place relation $L \subseteq X_1 \times ... \times X_k$ is one of the sets X_j, $1 \leq j \leq k$. In the special case where k = 2 and $L \subseteq X_1 \times X_2$ is a function $L : X_1 \to X_2$, it is conventional to refer to X_1 as the _____ of the function and to refer to X_2 as the codomain of the function.
   a. Domain0
   b. Thing
   c. Undefined
   d. Undefined

148. In geometry, _____ are plane figures that are bounded by a closed path or circuit, composed of a finite number of sequential line segments.
   a. Polygons0
   b. Thing
   c. Undefined
   d. Undefined

149. An _____ is a polygon that has eight sides.
   a. Thing
   b. Octagon0
   c. Undefined
   d. Undefined

Chapter 6. More Group Theory

1. The _____, the average in everyday English, which is also called the arithmetic _____ (and is distinguished from the geometric _____ or harmonic _____). The average is also called the sample _____. The expected value of a random variable, which is also called the population _____.
   - a. Mean0
   - b. Thing
   - c. Undefined
   - d. Undefined

2. _____ was an English mathematician.
   - a. Thing
   - b. James Joseph Sylvester0
   - c. Undefined
   - d. Undefined

3. _____ is the rearrangement of objects or symbols into distinguishable sequences.
   - a. Thing
   - b. Permutation0
   - c. Undefined
   - d. Undefined

4. In mathematics, a _____ is a statement that can be proved on the basis of explicitly stated or previously agreed assumptions.
   - a. Thing
   - b. Theorem0
   - c. Undefined
   - d. Undefined

5. In mathematics, a set is called _____ if there is a bijection between the set and some set of the form {1, 2, ..., n} where n is a natural number.
   - a. Thing
   - b. Finite0
   - c. Undefined
   - d. Undefined

6. In mathematics, an _____ (Greek:isos "equal", and morphe "shape") is a bijective map f such that both f and its inverse f $^{-1}$ are homomorphisms, i.e. *structure-preserving* mappings.
   - a. Isomorphism0
   - b. Thing
   - c. Undefined
   - d. Undefined

7. In mathematics, a _____ is a demonstration that, assuming certain axioms, some statement is necessarily true.
   - a. Thing
   - b. Proof0
   - c. Undefined
   - d. Undefined

8. In group theory, given a group G under a binary operation *, we say that some subset H of G is a _____ of G if H also forms a group under the operation *.
   - a. Thing
   - b. Subgroup0
   - c. Undefined
   - d. Undefined

9. An _____ or member of a set is an object that when collected together make up the set.
   - a. Element0
   - b. Thing
   - c. Undefined
   - d. Undefined

10. In mathematics, the _____, or members of a set or more generally a class are all those objects which when collected together make up the set or class.
    - a. Thing
    - b. Elements0
    - c. Undefined
    - d. Undefined

Chapter 6. More Group Theory

11. In physics, an _____ is the path that an object makes around another object while under the influence of a source of centripetal force, such as gravity.
    a. Orbit0
    b. Thing
    c. Undefined
    d. Undefined

12. In algebra, a _____ is a binomial formed by taking the opposite of the second term of a binomial.
    a. Conjugate0
    b. Thing
    c. Undefined
    d. Undefined

13. _____ is the mathematical action of repeatedly adding or subtracting one, usually to find out how many objects there are or to set aside a desired number of objects.
    a. Thing
    b. Counting0
    c. Undefined
    d. Undefined

14. In set theory and its applications throughout mathematics, _____ are a collection of sets (or sometimes other mathematical objects) that can be unambiguously defined by a property that all its members share.
    a. Thing
    b. Classes0
    c. Undefined
    d. Undefined

15. Generally, a _____ is a splitting of something into parts.
    a. Partition0
    b. Thing
    c. Undefined
    d. Undefined

16. An _____ is an equality that remains true regardless of the values of any variables that appear within it, to distinguish it from an equality which is true under more particular conditions.
    a. Thing
    b. Identity0
    c. Undefined
    d. Undefined

17. In mathematics, an _____ (or neutral element) is a special type of element of a set with respect to a binary operation on that set.
    a. Concept
    b. Identity element0
    c. Undefined
    d. Undefined

18. In mathematics, a _____ (also spelled reflexion) is a map that transforms an object into its mirror image.
    a. Concept
    b. Reflection0
    c. Undefined
    d. Undefined

19. A _____ is a movement of an object in a circular motion. A two-dimensional object rotates around a center (or point) of _____. A three-dimensional object rotates around a line called an axis. If the axis of _____ is within the body, the body is said to rotate upon itself, or spin—which implies relative speed and perhaps free-movement with angular momentum. A circular motion about an external point, e.g. the Earth about the Sun, is called an orbit or more properly an orbital revolution.
    a. Rotation0
    b. Thing
    c. Undefined
    d. Undefined

20. In geometry, the _____ of an object is a point in some sense in the middle of the object.

a. Center0 b. Thing
c. Undefined d. Undefined

21. _____ has many meanings, most of which simply .
a. Power0 b. Thing
c. Undefined d. Undefined

22. In mathematics, a _____ occurs if there is a bijection between the set and some set of the form 1, 2, ..., n where n is a natural number.
a. Finite set0 b. Concept
c. Undefined d. Undefined

23. In mathematics, a _____ of an integer n, also called a factor of n, is an integer which evenly divides n without leaving a remainder.
a. Divisor0 b. Thing
c. Undefined d. Undefined

24. In group theory, a _____ or monogenous group is a group that can be generated by a single element, in the sense that the group has an element g called a "generator" of the group such that, when written multiplicatively, every element of the group is a power of g a multiple of g when the notation is additive.
a. Thing b. Cyclic group0
c. Undefined d. Undefined

25. In geometry, a _____ is a special kind of point, usually a corner of a polygon, polyhedron, or higher dimensional polytope. In the geometry of curves a _____ is a point of where the first derivative of curvature is zero. In graph theory, a _____ is the fundamental unit out of which graphs are formed
a. Thing b. Vertex0
c. Undefined d. Undefined

26. In mathematics, the additive inverse, or _____ of a number n is the number that, when added to n, yields zero. The additive inverse of n is denoted −n. For example, 7 is −7, because 7 + (−7) = 0, and the additive inverse of −0.3 is 0.3, because −0.3 + 0.3 = 0.
a. Opposite0 b. Thing
c. Undefined d. Undefined

27. In mathematics, the _____ of a number n is the number that, when added to n, yields zero. The _____ of n is denoted −n. For example, 7 is −7, because 7 + (−7) = 0, and the _____ of −0.3 is 0.3, because −0.3 + 0.3 = 0.
a. Additive inverse0 b. Thing
c. Undefined d. Undefined

28. In mathematics, the _____ of two sets A and B is the set that contains all elements of A that also belong to B (or equivalently, all elements of B that also belong to A), but no other elements.
a. Thing b. Intersection0
c. Undefined d. Undefined

Chapter 6. More Group Theory

29. A _____ fraction is a fraction in which the absolute value of the numerator is less than the denominator--hence, the absolute value of the fraction is less than 1.
    a. Proper0
    b. Thing
    c. Undefined
    d. Undefined

30. In mathematics, a _____ is a group which is not the trivial group and whose only normal subgroups are the trivial group and the group itself.
    a. Simple group0
    b. Thing
    c. Undefined
    d. Undefined

31. In mathematics, a _____ number (or a _____) is a natural number that has exactly two (distinct) natural number divisors, which are 1 and the _____ number itself.
    a. Prime0
    b. Thing
    c. Undefined
    d. Undefined

32. In set theory and other branches of mathematics, the _____ of a collection of sets is the set that contains everything that belongs to any of the sets, but nothing else.
    a. Union0
    b. Thing
    c. Undefined
    d. Undefined

33. A _____ is the result of the addition of a set of numbers. The numbers may be natural numbers, complex numbers, matrices, or still more complicated objects. An infinite _____ is a subtle procedure known as a series.
    a. Sum0
    b. Thing
    c. Undefined
    d. Undefined

34. A _____ is a three-dimensional solid object bounded by six square faces, facets, or sides, with three meeting at each vertex.
    a. Cube0
    b. Thing
    c. Undefined
    d. Undefined

35. _____ are of a number n in its third power-the result of multiplying it by itself three times.
    a. Cubes0
    b. Thing
    c. Undefined
    d. Undefined

36. A _____ is any polyhedron with twelve faces, but usually a regular _____ is meant: a Platonic solid composed of twelve regular pentagonal faces, with three meeting at each vertex.
    a. Dodecahedron0
    b. Thing
    c. Undefined
    d. Undefined

37. In abstract algebra, a _____ is a structure-preserving map between two algebraic structures. The word _____ comes from the Greek language: homo meaning "same" and morphi meaning "shape".
    a. Homomorphism0
    b. Thing
    c. Undefined
    d. Undefined

38. In category theory and its applications to other branches of mathematics, _____ are a generalization of the kernels of group homomorphisms and the kernels of module homomorphisms and certain other kernels from algebra.

Chapter 6. More Group Theory

    a. Kernel0
    b. Thing
    c. Undefined
    d. Undefined

39. A _____ is a set whose members are members of another set or a set contained within another set.
    a. Thing
    b. Subset0
    c. Undefined
    d. Undefined

40. _____ are groups whose members are members of another set or a set contained within another set.
    a. Thing
    b. Subsets0
    c. Undefined
    d. Undefined

41. An _____ is any starting assumption from which other statements are logically derived
    a. Thing
    b. Axiom0
    c. Undefined
    d. Undefined

42. In mathematics, _____ is an elementary arithmetic operation. When one of the numbers is a whole number, _____ is the repeated sum of the other number.
    a. Multiplication0
    b. Thing
    c. Undefined
    d. Undefined

43. In mathematics, the conjugate _____ or adjoint matrix of an m-by-n matrix A with complex entries is the n-by-m matrix A* obtained from A by taking the transpose and then taking the complex conjugate of each entry.
    a. Pairs0
    b. Thing
    c. Undefined
    d. Undefined

44. A _____ is one of the basic shapes of geometry: a polygon with three vertices and three sides which are straight line segments.
    a. Thing
    b. Triangle0
    c. Undefined
    d. Undefined

45. _____ means "constancy", i.e. if something retains a certain feature even after we change a way of looking at it, then it is symmetric.
    a. Symmetry0
    b. Thing
    c. Undefined
    d. Undefined

46. In geometry, an _____ polygon is a polygon which has all sides of the same length.
    a. Thing
    b. Equilateral0
    c. Undefined
    d. Undefined

47. An _____ is a triangle in which all sides are of equal length.
    a. Equilateral triangle0
    b. Thing
    c. Undefined
    d. Undefined

48. In mathematics, the _____ of order 2n is the abstract group of which one representation is the symmetry group in 2D of a regular polygon with n sides

Chapter 6. More Group Theory

a. Dihedral group0
c. Undefined
b. Thing
d. Undefined

49. In mathematics, if G is a group, H a subgroup of G, and g an element of G, then, gH = {gh : h an element of H } is a left _____ of H in G, and Hg = {hg : h an element of H } is a right _____ of H in G.
   a. Coset0
   b. Thing
   c. Undefined
   d. Undefined

50. The word _____ is used in a variety of ways in mathematics.
   a. Index0
   b. Thing
   c. Undefined
   d. Undefined

51. _____ is a natural number that has exactly two distinct natural number divisors, which are 1 and the _____ itself.
   a. Thing
   b. Prime number0
   c. Undefined
   d. Undefined

52. In mathematics, the _____ of a function is the set of all "output" values produced by that function. Given a function $f : A \to B$, the _____ of f, is defined to be the set $\{x \in B : x = f(a) \text{ for some } a \in A\}$.
   a. Range0
   b. Thing
   c. Undefined
   d. Undefined

53. A _____ is a mathematical statement which follows easily from a previously proven statement, typically a mathematical theorem.
   a. Thing
   b. Corollary0
   c. Undefined
   d. Undefined

54. In mathematics, a _____ is the result of multiplying, or an expression that identifies factors to be multiplied.
   a. Product0
   b. Thing
   c. Undefined
   d. Undefined

55. Statistical _____ is a statistical procedure in which individual items are placed into groups based on quantitative information on one or more characteristics inherent in the items and based on a training set of previously labeled items.
   a. Thing
   b. Classification0
   c. Undefined
   d. Undefined

56. In mathematics, factorization (British English: factorisation) or factoring is the decomposition of an object (for example, a number, a polynomial, or a matrix) into a product of other objects, or _____, which when multiplied together give the original.
   a. Factors0
   b. Thing
   c. Undefined
   d. Undefined

57. In geometry, two sets are called _____ if one can be transformed into the other by an isometry, i.e., a combination of translations, rotations and reflections.

Chapter 6. More Group Theory

    a. Thing
    b. Congruent0
    c. Undefined
    d. Undefined

58. In mathematics and logic, a _____ proof is a way of showing the truth or falsehood of a given statement by a straightforward combination of established facts, usually existing lemmas and theorems, without making any further assumptions.
    a. Thing
    b. Direct0
    c. Undefined
    d. Undefined

59. _____ is a mathematical operation, written a^n, involving two numbers, the base a and the exponent n.
    a. Exponentiating0
    b. Thing
    c. Undefined
    d. Undefined

60. _____ is a mathematical operation, written a^n, involving two numbers, the base a and the exponent n.
    a. Thing
    b. Exponentiation0
    c. Undefined
    d. Undefined

61. In mathematics, a _____ is a constant multiplicative factor of a certain object. The object can be such things as a variable, a vector, a function, etc. For example, the _____ of $9x^2$ is 9.
    a. Thing
    b. Coefficient0
    c. Undefined
    d. Undefined

62. In elementary algebra, a _____ is a polynomial with two terms: the sum of two monomials. It is the simplest kind of polynomial except for a monomial.
    a. Thing
    b. Binomial0
    c. Undefined
    d. Undefined

63. In mathematics, particularly in combinatorics, the _____ of the natural number n and the integer k is the number of combinations that exist.
    a. Thing
    b. Binomial coefficient0
    c. Undefined
    d. Undefined

64. A _____ is a numeral used to indicate a count. The most common use of the word today is to name the part of a fraction that tells the number or count of equal parts.
    a. Numerator0
    b. Thing
    c. Undefined
    d. Undefined

65. A _____ is the part of a fraction that tells how many equal parts make up a whole, and which is used in the name of the fraction: "halves", "thirds", "fourths" or "quarters", "fifths" and so on.
    a. Denominator0
    b. Concept
    c. Undefined
    d. Undefined

66. Mathematical _____ is used to represent ideas.
    a. Thing
    b. Notation0
    c. Undefined
    d. Undefined

Chapter 6. More Group Theory

67. A _____, is a symbolized depiction of space which highlights relations between components of that space. Most usually a _____ is a two-dimensional, geometrically accurate representation of a three-dimensional space.
    a. Map0
    b. Thing
    c. Undefined
    d. Undefined

68. In mathematics, the term _____ is applied to certain functions. There are two common ways it is applied: these are related historically, but diverged somewhat during the twentieth century.
    a. Functional0
    b. Thing
    c. Undefined
    d. Undefined

69. In linear algebra, the _____ of a matrix A is another matrix AT
    a. Thing
    b. Transpose0
    c. Undefined
    d. Undefined

70. In physics and in _____ calculus, a spatial _____, or simply _____, is a concept characterized by a magnitude and a direction.
    a. Thing
    b. Vector0
    c. Undefined
    d. Undefined

71. In mathematics, a _____ is a rectangular table of numbers or, more generally, a table consisting of abstract quantities that can be added and multiplied.
    a. Thing
    b. Matrix0
    c. Undefined
    d. Undefined

72. In linear algebra, a _____ is a 1 × n matrix, that is, a matrix consisting of a single row
    a. Thing
    b. Row vector0
    c. Undefined
    d. Undefined

73. _____ are objects, characters, or other concrete representations of ideas, concepts, or other abstractions.
    a. Thing
    b. Symbols0
    c. Undefined
    d. Undefined

74. In informal language, a _____ is a function that swaps two elements of a set.
    a. Thing
    b. Transposition0
    c. Undefined
    d. Undefined

75. In mathematics, two sets are said to be _____ if they have no element in common. For example, {1, 2, 3} and {4, 5, 6} are sets which are _____.
    a. Thing
    b. Disjoint0
    c. Undefined
    d. Undefined

76. A _____ is 360° or 2ð radians.
    a. Turn0
    b. Thing
    c. Undefined
    d. Undefined

Chapter 6. More Group Theory

77. In mathematics, the idea of _____ generalises the concepts of negation, in relation to addition, and reciprocal, in relation to multiplication.
   a. Thing
   b. Inverse element0
   c. Undefined
   d. Undefined

78. In mathematics, a _____ function in the sense of algebraic geometry is an everywhere-defined, polynomial function on an algebraic variety V with values in the field K over which V is defined.
   a. Thing
   b. Regular0
   c. Undefined
   d. Undefined

79. A _____ consists either of a suggested explanation for a phenomenon or of a reasoned proposal suggesting a possible correlation between multiple phenomena.
   a. Hypothesis0
   b. Thing
   c. Undefined
   d. Undefined

80. Two mathematical objects are equal if and only if they are precisely the same in every way. This defines a binary relation, _____, denoted by the sign of _____ "=" in such a way that the statement "x = y" means that x and y are equal.
   a. Thing
   b. Equality0
   c. Undefined
   d. Undefined

81. In mathematics, suppose C is a collection of mathematical objects . Then we say that C is _____ if every c , C is uniquely determined by less information about c than one would expect.
   a. Rigid0
   b. Thing
   c. Undefined
   d. Undefined

82. In Euclidean mathematics, _____ consists of a transformation of the plane or space, which preserves distance and angles.
   a. Rigid motion0
   b. Thing
   c. Undefined
   d. Undefined

83. In mathematics, a _____ is a two-dimensional manifold or surface that is perfectly flat.
   a. Thing
   b. Plane0
   c. Undefined
   d. Undefined

84. A _____ in mathematics, is a group G is called free if there is a subset S of G such that ny element of G can be written in one and only one way as a product of finitely many elements of S and their inverses.
   a. Free group0
   b. Thing
   c. Undefined
   d. Undefined

85. In financial mathematics, the _____ volatility of an option contract is the volatility _____ by the market price of the option based on an option pricing model.
   a. Implied0
   b. Thing
   c. Undefined
   d. Undefined

86. _____ is the state of being greater than any finite real or natural number, however large.

Chapter 6. More Group Theory

a. Thing
b. Infinite0
c. Undefined
d. Undefined

87. _____ is a property that a binary operation can have.
    a. Associative law0
    b. Thing
    c. Undefined
    d. Undefined

88. In mathematics, a _____ of a positive integer n is a way of writing n as a sum of positive integers.
    a. Composition0
    b. Thing
    c. Undefined
    d. Undefined

89. In mathematics, the notion of _____ is a generalization of the notion of invertible.
    a. Cancellation0
    b. Thing
    c. Undefined
    d. Undefined

90. In mathematics, a _____ is an ordered list of objects. Like a set, it contains members, also called elements or terms, and the number of terms is called the length of the _____. Unlike a set, order matters, and the exact same elements can appear multiple times at different positions in the _____.
    a. Thing
    b. Sequence0
    c. Undefined
    d. Undefined

91. In mathematics and more specifically set theory, the _____ set is the unique set which contains no elements.
    a. Thing
    b. Empty0
    c. Undefined
    d. Undefined

92. Equivalence is the condition of being _____ or essentially equal.
    a. Thing
    b. Equivalent0
    c. Undefined
    d. Undefined

93. A _____ is a negotiable instrument instructing a financial institution to pay a specific amount of a specific currency from a specific demand account held in the maker/depositor's name with that institution. Both the maker and payee may be natural persons or legal entities.
    a. Thing
    b. Check0
    c. Undefined
    d. Undefined

94. In mathematics, a _____ is the end result of a division problem. It can also be expressed as the number of times the divisor divides into the dividend.
    a. Quotient0
    b. Thing
    c. Undefined
    d. Undefined

95. In mathematics, the _____ gives an indication of the extent to which a certain binary operation fails to be commutative. There are different definitions used in group theory and ring theory.
    a. Thing
    b. Commutator0
    c. Undefined
    d. Undefined

Chapter 6. More Group Theory

96. In mathematics, computing, linguistics, and related disciplines, an _____ is a finite list of well-defined instructions for accomplishing some task which, given an initial state, will terminate in a defined end-state.
   a. Concept
   b. Algorithm0
   c. Undefined
   d. Undefined

97. _____ the expected value of a random variable displays the average or central value of the variable. It is a summary value of the distribution of the variable.
   a. Determining0
   b. Thing
   c. Undefined
   d. Undefined

98. _____ element of an element x with respect to a binary operation * with identity element e is an element y such that x * y = y * x = e. In particular,
   a. Thing
   b. Inverse0
   c. Undefined
   d. Undefined

99. In mathematics, a _____ is a result saying that a function F will have at least one fixed point, under some conditions on F that can be stated in general terms.
   a. Thing
   b. Fixed point theorem0
   c. Undefined
   d. Undefined

100. In mathematics, an _____, also called a commutative group, is a group such that a * b= b*a for all and b in G. In other words, the order in which the binary operation is performed doesnt matter.
   a. Abelian group0
   b. Thing
   c. Undefined
   d. Undefined

101. A _____ (plural: tetrahedra) is a polyhedron composed of four triangular faces, three of which meet at each vertex.
   a. Tetrahedron0
   b. Thing
   c. Undefined
   d. Undefined

102. A _____ can refer to a line joining two nonadjacent vertices of a polygon or polyhedron, or in some contexts any upward or downward sloping line. .
   a. Diagonal0
   b. Thing
   c. Undefined
   d. Undefined

103. A _____ of a number is the product of that number with any integer.
   a. Multiple0
   b. Thing
   c. Undefined
   d. Undefined

104. The _____ of two integers is the smallest positive integer that is a multiple of both intergers.
   a. Least common multiple0
   b. Thing
   c. Undefined
   d. Undefined

105. _____ refers to the reduction of the body of a formerly living organism into simpler forms of matter.

Chapter 6. More Group Theory

a. Thing
b. Decomposing0
c. Undefined
d. Undefined

106. The _____ of a ring R is defined to be the smallest positive integer n such that n a = 0, for all a in R.
a. Characteristic0
b. Thing
c. Undefined
d. Undefined

107. _____ algebra (sometimes called General algebra) is the field of mathematics that studies the ideas common to all algebraic structures.
a. Universal0
b. Thing
c. Undefined
d. Undefined

108. In abstract algebra, a _____ group is an abelian that has a "basis" in the sense that every element of the group can be written in one and only one way as a finite linear combination of elements of the basis, with integer coefficient.
a. Free abelian0
b. Thing
c. Undefined
d. Undefined

109. The _____ are the only integral domain whose positive elements are well-ordered, and in which order is preserved by addition. Like the natural numbers, the _____ form a countably infinite set. The set of all _____ is usually denoted in mathematics by a boldface Z .
a. Thing
b. Integers0
c. Undefined
d. Undefined

110. _____ has one 90° internal angle a right angle.
a. Right triangle0
b. Thing
c. Undefined
d. Undefined

111. An _____ triange is a triangle with at least two sides of equal length.
a. Thing
b. Isosceles0
c. Undefined
d. Undefined

Chapter 7. Bilinear Forms

1. In mathematics, a _____ is the result of multiplying, or an expression that identifies factors to be multiplied.
   a. Product0
   b. Thing
   c. Undefined
   d. Undefined

2. In mathematics, a _____ is a rectangular table of numbers or, more generally, a table consisting of abstract quantities that can be added and multiplied.
   a. Matrix0
   b. Thing
   c. Undefined
   d. Undefined

3. In mathematics, the _____, also known as the scalar product, is a binary operation which takes two vectors over the real numbers R and returns a real-valued scalar quantity. It is the standard inner product of the Euclidean space.
   a. Thing
   b. Dot product0
   c. Undefined
   d. Undefined

4. In linear algebra, the _____ of a matrix A is another matrix AT
   a. Thing
   b. Transpose0
   c. Undefined
   d. Undefined

5. In logic and mathematics, logical _____ is a logical relation that holds between a set T of formulas and a formula B when every model (or interpretation or valuation) of T is also a model of B.
   a. Implication0
   b. Concept
   c. Undefined
   d. Undefined

6. In linear algebra, a _____ is a square matrix, A, that is equal to its transpose.
   a. Thing
   b. Symmetric Matrix0
   c. Undefined
   d. Undefined

7. In physics and in _____ calculus, a spatial _____, or simply _____, is a concept characterized by a magnitude and a direction.
   a. Vector0
   b. Thing
   c. Undefined
   d. Undefined

8. _____ is an adjective usually refering to being in the centre.
   a. Thing
   b. Central0
   c. Undefined
   d. Undefined

9. A _____ is a set of numbers that designate location in a given reference system, such as x,y in a planar _____ system or an x,y,z in a three-dimensional _____ system.
   a. Thing
   b. Coordinate0
   c. Undefined
   d. Undefined

10. The word _____ comes from the Latin word linearis, which means created by lines.
    a. Thing
    b. Linear0
    c. Undefined
    d. Undefined

11. In mathematics, a _____ on a vector space V over a field F is a mapping V × V → F which is linear in both arguments.

Chapter 7. Bilinear Forms

a. Bilinear form0
b. Thing
c. Undefined
d. Undefined

12. In mathematics, the idea of _____ generalises the concepts of negation, in relation to addition, and reciprocal, in relation to multiplication.
    a. Inverse element0
    b. Thing
    c. Undefined
    d. Undefined

13. An _____ is a square matrix which has an inverse.
    a. Invertible matrix0
    b. Thing
    c. Undefined
    d. Undefined

14. _____ also called natural basis or canonical basis of the n-dimensional Euclidean space Rn is the basis obtained by taking the n basis vectors
    a. Thing
    b. Standard basis0
    c. Undefined
    d. Undefined

15. An _____ is an equality that remains true regardless of the values of any variables that appear within it, to distinguish it from an equality which is true under more particular conditions.
    a. Identity0
    b. Thing
    c. Undefined
    d. Undefined

16. A _____ is 360° or 2∂ radians.
    a. Thing
    b. Turn0
    c. Undefined
    d. Undefined

17. A _____ is a mathematical statement which follows easily from a previously proven statement, typically a mathematical theorem.
    a. Thing
    b. Corollary0
    c. Undefined
    d. Undefined

18. _____ is a kind of property which exists as magnitude or multitude. It is among the basic classes of things along with quality, substance, change, and relation.
    a. Amount0
    b. Thing
    c. Undefined
    d. Undefined

19. Equivalence is the condition of being _____ or essentially equal.
    a. Thing
    b. Equivalent0
    c. Undefined
    d. Undefined

20. A _____ is a negotiable instrument instructing a financial institution to pay a specific amount of a specific currency from a specific demand account held in the maker/depositor's name with that institution. Both the maker and payee may be natural persons or legal entities.
    a. Thing
    b. Check0
    c. Undefined
    d. Undefined

Chapter 7. Bilinear Forms

21. _____ means "constancy", i.e. if something retains a certain feature even after we change a way of looking at it, then it is symmetric.
    a. Symmetry0
    b. Thing
    c. Undefined
    d. Undefined

22. _____ is a collection of objects called vectors that, informally speaking, may be scaled and added.
    a. Thing
    b. Vector space0
    c. Undefined
    d. Undefined

23. _____ is a set, with some particular properties and usually some additional structure, such as the operations of addition or multiplication, for instance.
    a. Space0
    b. Thing
    c. Undefined
    d. Undefined

24. In mathematics, a set is called _____ if there is a bijection between the set and some set of the form {1, 2, ..., n} where n is a natural number.
    a. Thing
    b. Finite0
    c. Undefined
    d. Undefined

25. In linear algebra, two vectors in an inner product space are _____ if they are orthogonal (their inner product is 0) and both of unit length (the norm of each is 1). A set of vectors which is pairwise _____ (any two vectors in it are _____) is called an _____ set. A basis which forms an _____ set is called an _____ basis.
    a. Thing
    b. Orthonormal0
    c. Undefined
    d. Undefined

26. In mathematics, a _____ is a demonstration that, assuming certain axioms, some statement is necessarily true.
    a. Proof0
    b. Thing
    c. Undefined
    d. Undefined

27. In mathematics, a _____ is a statement that can be proved on the basis of explicitly stated or previously agreed assumptions.
    a. Thing
    b. Theorem0
    c. Undefined
    d. Undefined

28. In algebra, a _____ is a function depending on *n* that associates a scalar, det(*A*), to every *n*×*n* square matrix *A*.
    a. Determinant0
    b. Thing
    c. Undefined
    d. Undefined

29. The _____ in a vacuum is an important physical constant denoted by the letter c for constant or the Latin word celeritas meaning "swiftness
    a. Speed of light0
    b. Thing
    c. Undefined
    d. Undefined

30. In mathematics, a _____ is a constant multiplicative factor of a certain object. The object can be such things as a variable, a vector, a function, etc. For example, the _____ of $9x^2$ is 9.

Chapter 7. Bilinear Forms

a. Thing
b. Coefficient0
c. Undefined
d. Undefined

31. _____ is electromagnetic radiation with a wavelength that is visible to the eye (visible _____) or, in a technical or scientific context, electromagnetic radiation of any wavelength.
a. Light0
b. Thing
c. Undefined
d. Undefined

32. _____, Greek for "knowledge of nature," is the branch of science concerned with the discovery and characterization of universal laws which govern matter, energy, space, and time.
a. Physics0
b. Thing
c. Undefined
d. Undefined

33. In mathematics, _____ is synonymous with perpendicular when used as a simple adjective that is not part of any longer phrase with a standard definition. It means at right angles. It comes from the Greek á½€Ï Î¸ÏŒÏ, orthos, meaning "straight", used by Euclid to mean right; and Î³Ï‰Î½Î¯Î± gonia, meaning angle. Two streets that cross each other at a right angle are _____ to one another.
a. Thing
b. Orthogonal0
c. Undefined
d. Undefined

34. In mathematics, the _____ (also nullspace) of an operator A is the set of all operands v which solve the equation Av = 0. It is also called the kernel of A.
a. Null space0
b. Thing
c. Undefined
d. Undefined

35. A _____ can refer to a line joining two nonadjacent vertices of a polygon or polyhedron, or in some contexts any upward or downward sloping line. .
a. Diagonal0
b. Thing
c. Undefined
d. Undefined

36. _____ is a square matrix in which the entries outside the main diagonal are all zero.
a. Diagonal matrix0
b. Thing
c. Undefined
d. Undefined

37. In mathematics, particularly linear algebra, a _____ is a matrix with all its entries being zero.
a. Thing
b. Zero matrix0
c. Undefined
d. Undefined

38. An _____ or member of a set is an object that when collected together make up the set.
a. Thing
b. Element0
c. Undefined
d. Undefined

39. In plane geometry, a _____ is a polygon with four equal sides, four right angles, and parallel opposite sides. In algebra, the _____ of a number is that number multiplied by itself.

a. Square0
b. Thing
c. Undefined
d. Undefined

40. _____ are elementary linear transformations on a matrix which preserve matrix equivalence.
   a. Thing
   b. Elementary row operations0
   c. Undefined
   d. Undefined

41. Elementary _____ are simple transformations which can be applied to a matrix without changing the linear system of equations that it represents.
   a. Thing
   b. Row operations0
   c. Undefined
   d. Undefined

42. In mathematics, a matrix can be thought of as each row or _____ being a vector. Hence, a space formed by row vectors or _____ vectors are said to be a row space or a _____ space.
   a. Column0
   b. Concept
   c. Undefined
   d. Undefined

43. _____ is bother the congnitive process of transferring information from a particular subject, and a linguistic expression corresponding to such a process.
   a. Analogy0
   b. Thing
   c. Undefined
   d. Undefined

44. _____ are objects, characters, or other concrete representations of ideas, concepts, or other abstractions.
   a. Symbols0
   b. Thing
   c. Undefined
   d. Undefined

45. The _____, the average in everyday English, which is also called the arithmetic _____ (and is distinguished from the geometric _____ or harmonic _____). The average is also called the sample _____. The expected value of a random variable, which is also called the population _____.
   a. Mean0
   b. Thing
   c. Undefined
   d. Undefined

46. A _____ is one of the basic shapes of geometry: a polygon with three vertices and three sides which are straight line segments.
   a. Thing
   b. Triangle0
   c. Undefined
   d. Undefined

47. _____ is the theorem stating that for any triangle, the measure of a given side must be less than the sum of the other two sides but greater than the difference between the two sides.
   a. Triangle inequality0
   b. Thing
   c. Undefined
   d. Undefined

Chapter 7. Bilinear Forms

48. Around 300 BC, the Greek mathematician Euclid laid down the rules of what has now come to be called "Euclidean geometry", which is the study of the relationships between angles and distances in space. Euclid first developed "plane geometry" which dealt with the geometry of two-dimensional objects on a flat surface. He then went on to develop "solid geometry" which analyzed the geometry of three-dimensional objects. All of the axioms of Euclid have been encoded into an abstract mathematical space known as a two- or three-dimensional _____. These mathematical spaces may be extended to apply to any dimension, and such a space is called an n-dimensional _____.
   a. Thing
   b. Euclidean space0
   c. Undefined
   d. Undefined

49. In mathematics, an _____ is a statement about the relative size or order of two objects.
   a. Thing
   b. Inequality0
   c. Undefined
   d. Undefined

50. In mathematics, a _____ is any one of several different types of functions, mappings, operations, or transformations.
   a. Thing
   b. Projection0
   c. Undefined
   d. Undefined

51. The _____ (symbol _____) and the millibar (symbol mbar, also mb) are units of pressure.
   a. Thing
   b. Bar0
   c. Undefined
   d. Undefined

52. A _____ is a symbolic representation denoting a quantity or expression. It often represents an "unknown" quantity that has the potential to change.
   a. Variable0
   b. Thing
   c. Undefined
   d. Undefined

53. _____ comes from the Latin word linearis, which means created by lines.
   a. Linearity0
   b. Thing
   c. Undefined
   d. Undefined

54. In algebra, a _____ is a binomial formed by taking the opposite of the second term of a binomial.
   a. Thing
   b. Conjugate0
   c. Undefined
   d. Undefined

55. In mathematics, an _____ is something that does not change under a set of transformations. The property of being an _____ is invariance.
   a. Invariant0
   b. Thing
   c. Undefined
   d. Undefined

56. Mathematical _____ are demonstrations that, assuming certain axioms, some statement is necessarily true.
   a. Proofs0
   b. Thing
   c. Undefined
   d. Undefined

57. An _____ of a linear transformation is a non-zero vector that is either left unaffected or simply multiplied by a scale factor after the transformation.

Chapter 7. Bilinear Forms

    a. Eigenvector0
    c. Undefined
    b. Thing
    d. Undefined

58. In mathematics, particularly linear algebra and functional analysis, the _____ is any of a number of results about linear operators or about matrices. In broad terms the _____ provides conditions under which an operator or a matrix can be diagonalized . This concept of diagonalization is relatively straightforward for operators on finite-dimensional spaces, but requires some modification for operators on infinite-dimensional spaces. In general, the _____ identifies a class of linear operators that can be modelled by multiplication operators, which are as simple as one can hope to find.
    a. Spectral theorem0
    c. Undefined
    b. Thing
    d. Undefined

59. A vector can be thought of as an arrow. It has a length, called its magnitude, and it points in some particular direction. A linear transformation inputs a vector and changes it, usually changing both its magnitude and its direction. An eigenvector of a given linear transformation is a vector which is simply multiplied by a constant called the _____ during that transformation.
    a. Thing
    c. Undefined
    b. Eigenvalue0
    d. Undefined

60. The _____ of a ring R is defined to be the smallest positive integer n such that $n\,a = 0$, for all a in R.
    a. Characteristic0
    c. Undefined
    b. Thing
    d. Undefined

61. In mathematics, a _____ may be described informally as a number that can be given by an infinite decimal representation.
    a. Real number0
    c. Undefined
    b. Thing
    d. Undefined

62. In mathematics, a _____ of a complex-valued function f is a member x of the domain of f such that f(x) vanishes at x, that is, x : f (x) = 0.
    a. Root0
    c. Undefined
    b. Thing
    d. Undefined

63. In mathematics, a _____ is an expression that is constructed from one or more variables and constants, using only the operations of addition, subtraction, multiplication, and constant positive whole number exponents. is a _____. Note in particular that division by an expression containing a variable is not in general allowed in polynomials. [1]
    a. Polynomial0
    c. Undefined
    b. Thing
    d. Undefined

64. In mathematics and more specifically set theory, the _____ set is the unique set which contains no elements.
    a. Empty0
    c. Undefined
    b. Thing
    d. Undefined

65. In mathematics, a _____ case is a limiting case in which a class of object changes its nature so as to belong to another, usually simpler, class.

Chapter 7. Bilinear Forms

a. Thing
c. Undefined
b. Degenerate0
d. Undefined

66. In mathematics, a conic section is a curve that can be formed by interesting a cone with a plane. _____ is when a plane passes through the apex of a cone.
   a. Thing
   c. Undefined
   b. Degenerate conic0
   d. Undefined

67. In mathematics, a _____ section is a curve that can be formed by intersecting a cone with a plane.
   a. Conic0
   c. Undefined
   b. Thing
   d. Undefined

68. In mathematics, a _____ is a homogeneous polynomial of degree two in a number of variables.
   a. Quadratic form0
   c. Undefined
   b. Thing
   d. Undefined

69. In mathematics, there are several meanings of _____ depending on the subject.
   a. Thing
   c. Undefined
   b. Degree0
   d. Undefined

70. Mathematical _____ is used to represent ideas.
   a. Thing
   c. Undefined
   b. Notation0
   d. Undefined

71. In set theory and its applications throughout mathematics, _____ are a collection of sets (or sometimes other mathematical objects) that can be unambiguously defined by a property that all its members share.
   a. Thing
   c. Undefined
   b. Classes0
   d. Undefined

72. _____ is an m × 1 matrix, i.e. a matrix consisting of a single column of m elements.
   a. Thing
   c. Undefined
   b. Column vector0
   d. Undefined

73. In physics, an _____ is the path that an object makes around another object while under the influence of a source of centripetal force, such as gravity.
   a. Orbit0
   c. Undefined
   b. Thing
   d. Undefined

74. In mathematics, suppose C is a collection of mathematical objects . Then we say that C is _____ if every c , C is uniquely determined by less information about c than one would expect.
   a. Thing
   c. Undefined
   b. Rigid0
   d. Undefined

75. In Euclidean mathematics, _____ consists of a transformation of the plane or space, which preserves distance and angles.

Chapter 7. Bilinear Forms

  a. Thing
  b. Rigid motion0
  c. Undefined
  d. Undefined

76. In linear algebra, a _____ is a 1 × n matrix, that is, a matrix consisting of a single row
  a. Thing
  b. Row vector0
  c. Undefined
  d. Undefined

77. In mathematics, a _____ is a two-dimensional manifold or surface that is perfectly flat.
  a. Thing
  b. Plane0
  c. Undefined
  d. Undefined

78. As an abstract term, _____ means similarity between objects.
  a. Congruence0
  b. Thing
  c. Undefined
  d. Undefined

79. In geometry, two sets are called _____ if one can be transformed into the other by an isometry, i.e., a combination of translations, rotations and reflections.
  a. Thing
  b. Congruent0
  c. Undefined
  d. Undefined

80. In mathematics and the mathematical sciences, a _____ is a fixed, but possibly unspecified, value. This is in contrast to a variable, which is not fixed.
  a. Constant0
  b. Thing
  c. Undefined
  d. Undefined

81. _____ is a fixed, but possibly unspecified, value. This is in contrast to a variable, which is not fixed.
  a. Constant term0
  b. Thing
  c. Undefined
  d. Undefined

82. In mathematics, an _____ .
  a. Ellipse0
  b. Thing
  c. Undefined
  d. Undefined

83. In mathematics, a _____ is a polynomial equation of the second degree. The general form is $ax^2 + bx + c = 0$.
  a. Quadratic equation0
  b. Thing
  c. Undefined
  d. Undefined

84. A _____ is the result of the addition of a set of numbers. The numbers may be natural numbers, complex numbers, matrices, or still more complicated objects. An infinite _____ is a subtle procedure known as a series.
  a. Thing
  b. Sum0
  c. Undefined
  d. Undefined

85. In mathematics, the conjugate _____ or adjoint matrix of an m-by-n matrix A with complex entries is the n-by-m matrix A* obtained from A by taking the transpose and then taking the complex conjugate of each entry.

Chapter 7. Bilinear Forms

a. Pairs0
b. Thing
c. Undefined
d. Undefined

86. In Euclidean geometry, a _____ is moving every point a constant distance in a specified direction.
    a. Concept
    b. Translation0
    c. Undefined
    d. Undefined

87. An _____ is a type of quadric surface that is a higher dimensional analogue of an ellipse.
    a. Thing
    b. Ellipsoid0
    c. Undefined
    d. Undefined

88. _____ is a quadric, a type of surface in three dimensions
    a. Thing
    b. Elliptic paraboloid0
    c. Undefined
    d. Undefined

89. _____ is a quadric
    a. Thing
    b. Paraboloid0
    c. Undefined
    d. Undefined

90. _____ is a quadric, a type of surface in three dimensions
    a. Thing
    b. Hyperbolic paraboloid0
    c. Undefined
    d. Undefined

91. In mathamatics, a _____ is a quadric, a type of surface in three dimensions, described by the equation
    a. Thing
    b. Hyperboloid0
    c. Undefined
    d. Undefined

92. _____ Logic is a concept in traditional logic referring to a "type of immediate inference in which from a given proposition another proposition is inferred which has as its subject the predicate of the original proposition and as its predicate the subject of the original proposition (the quality of the proposition being retained)."
    a. Concept
    b. Converse0
    c. Undefined
    d. Undefined

93. In linear algebra, real numbers are called scalars and relate to vectors in a vector space through the operation of _____ multiplication, in which a vector can be multiplied by a number to produce another vector.
    a. Scalar0
    b. Thing
    c. Undefined
    d. Undefined

94. _____ geometry is a branch of differential topology/geometry which studies _____ manifolds; that is, differentiable manifolds equipped with a closed, nondegenerate 2-form. _____ geometry has its origins in the Hamiltonian formulation of classical mechanics where the phase space of certain classical systems takes on the structure of a _____ manifold.
    a. Symplectic0
    b. Thing
    c. Undefined
    d. Undefined

Chapter 7. Bilinear Forms

95. The _____ are the only integral domain whose positive elements are well-ordered, and in which order is preserved by addition. Like the natural numbers, the _____ form a countably infinite set. The set of all _____ is usually denoted in mathematics by a boldface Z .
   a. Thing
   b. Integers0
   c. Undefined
   d. Undefined

96. In mathematics, a _____ is a number in the form of a + bi where a and b are real numbers, and i is the imaginary unit, with the property i 2 = −1. The real number a is called the real part of the _____, and the real number b is the imaginary part.
   a. Thing
   b. Complex number0
   c. Undefined
   d. Undefined

97. In mathematics, a _____ in elementary terms is any of a variety of different functions from geometry, such as rotations, reflections and translations.
   a. Transformation0
   b. Thing
   c. Undefined
   d. Undefined

98. In mathematics, a linear map also called a _____ or linear operator is a function between two vector spaces that preserves the operations of vector addition and scalar multiplication.
   a. Linear transformation0
   b. Thing
   c. Undefined
   d. Undefined

99. The mathematical concept of a _____ expresses the intuitive idea of deterministic dependence between two quantities, one of which is viewed as primary and the other as secondary. A _____ then is a way to associate a unique output for each input of a specified type, for example, a real number or an element of a given set.
   a. Function0
   b. Thing
   c. Undefined
   d. Undefined

100. In linear algebra, the _____ of an n-by-n square matrix A is defined to be the sum of the elements on the main diagonal of A,
   a. Trace0
   b. Thing
   c. Undefined
   d. Undefined

101. The _____ is a useful inequality encountered in many different settings, such as linear algebra applied to vectors, in analysis applied to infinite series and integration of products, and in probability theory, applied to variances and covariances.
   a. Thing
   b. Buniakowsky inequality0
   c. Undefined
   d. Undefined

102. In geometry, an _____ polygon is a polygon which has all sides of the same length.
   a. Thing
   b. Equilateral0
   c. Undefined
   d. Undefined

103. An _____ is a triangle in which all sides are of equal length.

Chapter 7. Bilinear Forms

a. Thing
c. Undefined
b. Equilateral triangle0
d. Undefined

104. In mathematics, _____ is a part of the set theoretic notion of function.
a. Image0
c. Undefined
b. Thing
d. Undefined

105. In mathematics, _____ is an elementary arithmetic operation. When one of the numbers is a whole number, _____ is the repeated sum of the other number.
a. Multiplication0
c. Undefined
b. Thing
d. Undefined

106. In mathematics, a _____ (also spelled reflexion) is a map that transforms an object into its mirror image.
a. Concept
c. Undefined
b. Reflection0
d. Undefined

107. In mathematics, the _____ of a complex number z, is the first element of the ordered pair of real numbers representing z, i.e. if z = (x,y), or equivalently, z = x + iy, then the _____ of z is x. It is denoted by Re{z} . The complex function which maps z to the _____ of z is not holomorphic.
a. Real part0
c. Undefined
b. Thing
d. Undefined

108. _____ is a mathematical subject that includes the study of limits, derivatives, integrals, and power series and constitutes a major part of modern university curriculum.
a. Thing
c. Undefined
b. Calculus0
d. Undefined

109. In Euclidean geometry, a _____ is the set of all points in a plane at a fixed distance, called the radius, from a given point, the center.
a. Circle0
c. Undefined
b. Thing
d. Undefined

110. In mathematics, the _____ (or modulus) of a real number is its numerical value without regard to its sign.
a. Absolute value0
c. Undefined
b. Thing
d. Undefined

111. In mathematics, an _____ number is a complex number whose square is a negative real number. They were defined in 1572 by Rafael Bombelli.
a. Imaginary0
c. Undefined
b. Thing
d. Undefined

112. _____ element of an element x with respect to a binary operation * with identity element e is an element y such that x * y = y * x = e. In particular,
a. Inverse0
c. Undefined
b. Thing
d. Undefined

113. A _____ is a movement of an object in a circular motion. A two-dimensional object rotates around a center (or point) of _____. A three-dimensional object rotates around a line called an axis. If the axis of _____ is within the body, the body is said to rotate upon itself, or spin—which implies relative speed and perhaps free-movement with angular momentum. A circular motion about an external point, e.g. the Earth about the Sun, is called an orbit or more properly an orbital revolution.
- a. Thing
- b. Rotation0
- c. Undefined
- d. Undefined

114. In mathematics, _____ are two-dimensional manifolds or surfaces that are perfectly flat.
- a. Thing
- b. Planes0
- c. Undefined
- d. Undefined

Chapter 8. Linear Groups

1. In group theory, given a group G under a binary operation *, we say that some subset H of G is a _____ of G if H also forms a group under the operation *.
   - a. Subgroup0
   - b. Thing
   - c. Undefined
   - d. Undefined

2. _____ was a German mathematician. Although much of his working life was spent in Zürich and then Princeton, he is closely identified with the University of Göttingen tradition of mathematics, represented by David Hilbert and Hermann Minkowski. His research has had major significance for theoretical physics as well as pure disciplines including number theory. He was one of the most influential mathematicians of the twentieth century, and a key member of the Institute for Advanced Study in its early years, in terms of creating an integrated and international view.
   - a. Person
   - b. Hermann Weyl0
   - c. Undefined
   - d. Undefined

3. The word _____ comes from the Latin word linearis, which means created by lines.
   - a. Thing
   - b. Linear0
   - c. Undefined
   - d. Undefined

4. _____ is a set, with some particular properties and usually some additional structure, such as the operations of addition or multiplication, for instance.
   - a. Space0
   - b. Thing
   - c. Undefined
   - d. Undefined

5. In mathematics, a _____ is a rectangular table of numbers or, more generally, a table consisting of abstract quantities that can be added and multiplied.
   - a. Thing
   - b. Matrix0
   - c. Undefined
   - d. Undefined

6. In physics, an _____ is the path that an object makes around another object while under the influence of a source of centripetal force, such as gravity.
   - a. Orbit0
   - b. Thing
   - c. Undefined
   - d. Undefined

7. In geometry, two sets are called _____ if one can be transformed into the other by an isometry, i.e., a combination of translations, rotations and reflections.
   - a. Congruent0
   - b. Thing
   - c. Undefined
   - d. Undefined

8. In mathematics, _____ is synonymous with perpendicular when used as a simple adjective that is not part of any longer phrase with a standard definition. It means at right angles. It comes from the Greek á½€Ï̧ÏŒÏ, orthos, meaning "straight", used by Euclid to mean right; and Î³Ï‰Î½Î¯Î± gonia, meaning angle. Two streets that cross each other at a right angle are _____ to one another.
   - a. Orthogonal0
   - b. Thing
   - c. Undefined
   - d. Undefined

9. An _____ is an equality that remains true regardless of the values of any variables that appear within it, to distinguish it from an equality which is true under more particular conditions.

a. Identity0
b. Thing
c. Undefined
d. Undefined

10. As an abstract term, _____ means similarity between objects.
   a. Congruence0
   b. Thing
   c. Undefined
   d. Undefined

11. In mathematics, a _____ in elementary terms is any of a variety of different functions from geometry, such as rotations, reflections and translations.
   a. Transformation0
   b. Thing
   c. Undefined
   d. Undefined

12. A _____ is a number, figure, or indicator that appears below the normal line of type, typically used in a formula, mathematical expression, or description of a chemical compound.
   a. Thing
   b. Subscript0
   c. Undefined
   d. Undefined

13. In mathematics, a _____ on a vector space V over a field F is a mapping V × V → F which is linear in both arguments.
   a. Thing
   b. Bilinear form0
   c. Undefined
   d. Undefined

14. In algebra, a _____ is a function depending on n that associates a scalar, det(A), to every $n \times n$ square matrix A.
   a. Determinant0
   b. Thing
   c. Undefined
   d. Undefined

15. In mathematics, the _____ of two sets A and B is the set that contains all elements of A that also belong to B (or equivalently, all elements of B that also belong to A), but no other elements.
   a. Intersection0
   b. Thing
   c. Undefined
   d. Undefined

16. A _____ is the quantity that defines certain relatively constant characteristics of systems or functions..
   a. Thing
   b. Parameter0
   c. Undefined
   d. Undefined

17. A _____ is a movement of an object in a circular motion. A two-dimensional object rotates around a center (or point) of _____. A three-dimensional object rotates around a line called an axis. If the axis of _____ is within the body, the body is said to rotate upon itself, or spinâ€"which implies relative speed and perhaps free-movement with angular momentum. A circular motion about an external point, e.g. the Earth about the Sun, is called an orbit or more properly an orbital revolution.
   a. Thing
   b. Rotation0
   c. Undefined
   d. Undefined

18. In mathematics, there are several meanings of _____ depending on the subject.

a. Thing
b. Degree0
c. Undefined
d. Undefined

19. An _____ or member of a set is an object that when collected together make up the set.
    a. Thing
    b. Element0
    c. Undefined
    d. Undefined

20. In mathematics, a _____ is the set of all points in three-dimensional space (R^3) which are at distance r from a fixed point of that space, where r is a positive real number called the radius of the _____. The fixed point is called the center or centre, and is not part of the _____ itself.
    a. Sphere0
    b. Thing
    c. Undefined
    d. Undefined

21. In mathematics, a _____ is a collection of points which share a property.
    a. Thing
    b. Locus0
    c. Undefined
    d. Undefined

22. _____ is bother the congnitive process of transferring information from a particular subject, and a linguistic expression corresponding to such a process.
    a. Thing
    b. Analogy0
    c. Undefined
    d. Undefined

23. _____ is a circle with a unit radius, i.e., a circle whose radius is 1.
    a. Unit circle0
    b. Thing
    c. Undefined
    d. Undefined

24. In Euclidean geometry, a _____ is the set of all points in a plane at a fixed distance, called the radius, from a given point, the center.
    a. Circle0
    b. Thing
    c. Undefined
    d. Undefined

25. In mathematics, the concept of a _____ tries to capture the intuitive idea of a geometrical one-dimensional and continuous object. A simple example is the circle.
    a. Curve0
    b. Thing
    c. Undefined
    d. Undefined

26. In the mathematical field of topology a _____ or topological isomorphism is a special isomorphism between topological spaces which respects topological properties.
    a. Thing
    b. Homeomorphism0
    c. Undefined
    d. Undefined

27. A _____ function is a function for which, intuitively, small changes in the input result in small changes in the output.
    a. Event
    b. Continuous0
    c. Undefined
    d. Undefined

Chapter 8. Linear Groups

28. In mathematics, a _____ of a positive integer n is a way of writing n as a sum of positive integers.
    a. Composition0
    b. Thing
    c. Undefined
    d. Undefined

29. In physics and in _____ calculus, a spatial _____, or simply _____, is a concept characterized by a magnitude and a direction.
    a. Thing
    b. Vector0
    c. Undefined
    d. Undefined

30. Mathematical _____ is used to represent ideas.
    a. Notation0
    b. Thing
    c. Undefined
    d. Undefined

31. _____, usually denoted symbolically by the Greek letter phi, Î¦, gives the location of a place on Earth north or south of the equator. _____ is an angular measurement in degrees (marked with Â°) ranging from 0Â° at the Equator (low _____) to 90Â° at the poles (90Â° N for the North Pole or 90Â° S for the South Pole; high _____). The complementary angle of a _____ is called the colatitude.
    a. Latitude0
    b. Thing
    c. Undefined
    d. Undefined

32. In mathematics and the mathematical sciences, a _____ is a fixed, but possibly unspecified, value. This is in contrast to a variable, which is not fixed.
    a. Constant0
    b. Thing
    c. Undefined
    d. Undefined

33. In set theory and its applications throughout mathematics, _____ are a collection of sets (or sometimes other mathematical objects) that can be unambiguously defined by a property that all its members share.
    a. Classes0
    b. Thing
    c. Undefined
    d. Undefined

34. In elementary algebra, an _____ is a set that contains every real number between two indicated numbers and may contain the two numbers themselves.
    a. Thing
    b. Interval0
    c. Undefined
    d. Undefined

35. In linear algebra, the _____ of an n-by-n square matrix A is defined to be the sum of the elements on the main diagonal of A,
    a. Trace0
    b. Thing
    c. Undefined
    d. Undefined

36. The _____ of a ring R is defined to be the smallest positive integer n such that $n\, a = 0$, for all a in R.
    a. Thing
    b. Characteristic0
    c. Undefined
    d. Undefined

Chapter 8. Linear Groups

37. A vector can be thought of as an arrow. It has a length, called its magnitude, and it points in some particular direction. A linear transformation inputs a vector and changes it, usually changing both its magnitude and its direction. An eigenvector of a given linear transformation is a vector which is simply multiplied by a constant called the _____ during that transformation.
   a. Thing
   b. Eigenvalue0
   c. Undefined
   d. Undefined

38. In mathematics, a _____ of a complex-valued function f is a member x of the domain of f such that f(x) vanishes at x, that is, x : f (x) = 0.
   a. Thing
   b. Root0
   c. Undefined
   d. Undefined

39. In mathematics, a _____ is an expression that is constructed from one or more variables and constants, using only the operations of addition, subtraction, multiplication, and constant positive whole number exponents. is a _____. Note in particular that division by an expression containing a variable is not in general allowed in polynomials. [1]
   a. Thing
   b. Polynomial0
   c. Undefined
   d. Undefined

40. In algebra, a _____ is a binomial formed by taking the opposite of the second term of a binomial.
   a. Thing
   b. Conjugate0
   c. Undefined
   d. Undefined

41. In mathematics, a _____ is a demonstration that, assuming certain axioms, some statement is necessarily true.
   a. Thing
   b. Proof0
   c. Undefined
   d. Undefined

42. In mathematics, particularly linear algebra and functional analysis, the _____ is any of a number of results about linear operators or about matrices. In broad terms the _____ provides conditions under which an operator or a matrix can be diagonalized . This concept of diagonalization is relatively straightforward for operators on finite-dimensional spaces, but requires some modification for operators on infinite-dimensional spaces. In general, the _____ identifies a class of linear operators that can be modelled by multiplication operators, which are as simple as one can hope to find.
   a. Thing
   b. Spectral theorem0
   c. Undefined
   d. Undefined

43. In mathematics, a _____ is a statement that can be proved on the basis of explicitly stated or previously agreed assumptions.
   a. Thing
   b. Theorem0
   c. Undefined
   d. Undefined

44. A _____ can refer to a line joining two nonadjacent vertices of a polygon or polyhedron, or in some contexts any upward or downward sloping line. .
   a. Diagonal0
   b. Thing
   c. Undefined
   d. Undefined

45. _____ is a circle on the surface of a sphere that has the same circumference as the sphere, dividing the sphere into two equal hemispheres.

a. Great circle0
b. Thing
c. Undefined
d. Undefined

46. _____ describes the location of a place on Earth east or west of a north-south line called the Prime Meridian.
   a. Longitude0
   b. Thing
   c. Undefined
   d. Undefined

47. In mathematics, a _____ is a two-dimensional manifold or surface that is perfectly flat.
   a. Thing
   b. Plane0
   c. Undefined
   d. Undefined

48. In mathematics, a _____ is any one of several different types of functions, mappings, operations, or transformations.
   a. Projection0
   b. Thing
   c. Undefined
   d. Undefined

49. In mathematics, an _____ .
   a. Ellipse0
   b. Thing
   c. Undefined
   d. Undefined

50. An _____ is a type of quadric surface that is a higher dimensional analogue of an ellipse.
   a. Ellipsoid0
   b. Thing
   c. Undefined
   d. Undefined

51. A _____ is a symbolic representation denoting a quantity or expression. It often represents an "unknown" quantity that has the potential to change.
   a. Thing
   b. Variable0
   c. Undefined
   d. Undefined

52. In mathematics, if G is a group, H a subgroup of G, and g an element of G, then, gH = {gh : h an element of H } is a left _____ of H in G, and Hg = {hg : h an element of H } is a right _____ of H in G.
   a. Thing
   b. Coset0
   c. Undefined
   d. Undefined

53. In category theory and its applications to other branches of mathematics, _____ are a generalization of the kernels of group homomorphisms and the kernels of module homomorphisms and certain other kernels from algebra.
   a. Thing
   b. Kernel0
   c. Undefined
   d. Undefined

54. In mathematics, the _____ , or members of a set or more generally a class are all those objects which when collected together make up the set or class.
   a. Thing
   b. Elements0
   c. Undefined
   d. Undefined

55. In mathematics, the _____ of a coordinate system is the point where the axes of the system intersect.

Chapter 8. Linear Groups

a. Origin0
b. Thing
c. Undefined
d. Undefined

56. In mathematics, the conjugate _____ or adjoint matrix of an m-by-n matrix A with complex entries is the n-by-m matrix A* obtained from A by taking the transpose and then taking the complex conjugate of each entry.
a. Pairs0
b. Thing
c. Undefined
d. Undefined

57. A _____, is a symbolized depiction of space which highlights relations between components of that space. Most usually a _____ is a two-dimensional, geometrically accurate representation of a three-dimensional space.
a. Thing
b. Map0
c. Undefined
d. Undefined

58. _____ is a collection of objects called vectors that, informally speaking, may be scaled and added.
a. Vector space0
b. Thing
c. Undefined
d. Undefined

59. In mathematics, _____ is an elementary arithmetic operation. When one of the numbers is a whole number, _____ is the repeated sum of the other number.
a. Multiplication0
b. Thing
c. Undefined
d. Undefined

60. In mathematics, a _____ is the result of multiplying, or an expression that identifies factors to be multiplied.
a. Product0
b. Thing
c. Undefined
d. Undefined

61. _____ is a property that a binary operation can have.
a. Associative law0
b. Thing
c. Undefined
d. Undefined

62. In abstract algebra, a _____ is a structure-preserving map between two algebraic structures. The word _____ comes from the Greek language: homo meaning "same" and morphi meaning "shape".
a. Homomorphism0
b. Thing
c. Undefined
d. Undefined

63. In mathematics, the idea of _____ generalises the concepts of negation, in relation to addition, and reciprocal, in relation to multiplication.
a. Inverse element0
b. Thing
c. Undefined
d. Undefined

64. An _____ is a combination of numbers, operators, grouping symbols and/or free variables and bound variables arranged in a meaningful way which can be evaluated..
a. Expression0
b. Thing
c. Undefined
d. Undefined

Chapter 8. Linear Groups

65. In mathematics, the _____, also known as the scalar product, is a binary operation which takes two vectors over the real numbers R and returns a real-valued scalar quantity. It is the standard inner product of the Euclidean space.
    a. Dot product0
    b. Thing
    c. Undefined
    d. Undefined

66. A _____ given two distinct points A and B on the _____, is the set of points C on the line containing points A and B such that A is not strictly between C and B.
    a. Ray0
    b. Thing
    c. Undefined
    d. Undefined

67. In geometry and physics, _____ are half-lines that continue forever in one direction.
    a. Thing
    b. Rays0
    c. Undefined
    d. Undefined

68. In mathematics, a matrix can be thought of as each row or _____ being a vector. Hence, a space formed by row vectors or _____ vectors are said to be a row space or a _____ space.
    a. Concept
    b. Column0
    c. Undefined
    d. Undefined

69. _____ is an m × 1 matrix, i.e. a matrix consisting of a single column of m elements.
    a. Column vector0
    b. Thing
    c. Undefined
    d. Undefined

70. A _____ is a set of numbers that designate location in a given reference system, such as x,y in a planar _____ system or an x,y,z in a three-dimensional _____ system.
    a. Thing
    b. Coordinate0
    c. Undefined
    d. Undefined

71. In mathematics, _____ is a part of the set theoretic notion of function.
    a. Image0
    b. Thing
    c. Undefined
    d. Undefined

72. In mathematics, in the field of group theory, a _____ of a group is a quasisimple subnormal subgroup.
    a. Concept
    b. Component0
    c. Undefined
    d. Undefined

73. A _____ is a negotiable instrument instructing a financial institution to pay a specific amount of a specific currency from a specific demand account held in the maker/depositor's name with that institution. Both the maker and payee may be natural persons or legal entities.
    a. Thing
    b. Check0
    c. Undefined
    d. Undefined

74. In mathematics, a _____ may be described informally as a number that can be given by an infinite decimal representation.

Chapter 8. Linear Groups

a. Thing
b. Real number0
c. Undefined
d. Undefined

75. The _____ is a measurement of how a function changes when the values of its inputs change.
a. Derivative0
b. Thing
c. Undefined
d. Undefined

76. The mathematical concept of a _____ expresses the intuitive idea of deterministic dependence between two quantities, one of which is viewed as primary and the other as secondary. A _____ then is a way to associate a unique output for each input of a specified type, for example, a real number or an element of a given set.
a. Function0
b. Thing
c. Undefined
d. Undefined

77. In mathematics, the _____ inverse, or opposite, of a number n is the number that, when added to n, yields zero. The _____ inverse of n is denoted −n.
a. Additive0
b. Thing
c. Undefined
d. Undefined

78. A _____ is traditionally an infinitesimally small change in a variable.
a. Thing
b. Differential0
c. Undefined
d. Undefined

79. A _____ is a mathematical equation for an unknown function of one or several variables which relates the values of the function itself and of its derivatives of various orders.
a. Differential equation0
b. Thing
c. Undefined
d. Undefined

80. A _____ is 360° or 2δ radians.
a. Turn0
b. Thing
c. Undefined
d. Undefined

81. In mathematics, _____ growth occurs when the growth rate of a function is always proportional to the function's current size.
a. Exponential0
b. Thing
c. Undefined
d. Undefined

82. _____ element of an element x with respect to a binary operation * with identity element e is an element y such that x * y = y * x = e. In particular,
a. Thing
b. Inverse0
c. Undefined
d. Undefined

83. An _____ is a function which does the reverse of a given function.
a. Inverse function0
b. Thing
c. Undefined
d. Undefined

84. In linear algebra, the _____ of a matrix A is another matrix AT

Chapter 8. Linear Groups

   a. Thing
   c. Undefined
   b. Transpose0
   d. Undefined

85. _____ Logic is a concept in traditional logic referring to a "type of immediate inference in which from a given proposition another proposition is inferred which has as its subject the predicate of the original proposition and as its predicate the subject of the original proposition (the quality of the proposition being retained)."
   a. Converse0
   c. Undefined
   b. Concept
   d. Undefined

86. A _____ is a mathematical statement which follows easily from a previously proven statement, typically a mathematical theorem.
   a. Corollary0
   c. Undefined
   b. Thing
   d. Undefined

87. _____ of an object is its speed in a particular direction.
   a. Velocity0
   c. Undefined
   b. Thing
   d. Undefined

88. In trigonometry, the _____ is a function defined as $\tan x = \sin x / \cos x$. The function is so-named because it can be defined as the length of a certain segment of a _____ (in the geometric sense) to the unit circle. In plane geometry, a line is _____ to a curve, at some point, if both line and curve pass through the point with the same direction.
   a. Tangent0
   c. Undefined
   b. Thing
   d. Undefined

89. In calculus, the _____ is a formula for the derivative of the composite of two functions.
   a. Chain rule0
   c. Undefined
   b. Concept
   d. Undefined

90. In vector calculus, the _____ of a scalar field is a vector field which points in the direction of the greatest rate of increase of the scalar field, and whose magnitude is the greatest rate of change.
   a. Thing
   c. Undefined
   b. Gradient0
   d. Undefined

91. A _____ is a set whose members are members of another set or a set contained within another set.
   a. Subset0
   c. Undefined
   b. Thing
   d. Undefined

92. _____, a field in mathematics, is the study of how functions change when their inputs change. The primary object of study in _____ is the derivative.
   a. Differential calculus0
   c. Undefined
   b. Thing
   d. Undefined

93. The _____, the average in everyday English, which is also called the arithmetic _____ (and is distinguished from the geometric _____ or harmonic _____). The average is also called the sample _____. The expected value of a random variable, which is also called the population _____.

Chapter 8. Linear Groups

a. Mean0
b. Thing
c. Undefined
d. Undefined

94. An _____ of a product of sums expresses it as a sum of products by using the fact that multiplication distributes over addition.
a. Thing
b. Expansion0
c. Undefined
d. Undefined

95. In mathematics, a _____ is a constant multiplicative factor of a certain object. The object can be such things as a variable, a vector, a function, etc. For example, the _____ of $9x^2$ is 9.
a. Thing
b. Coefficient0
c. Undefined
d. Undefined

96. In combinatorial mathematics, a _____ is an un-ordered collection of unique elements.
a. Combination0
b. Concept
c. Undefined
d. Undefined

97. In mathematics, a _____ is a number in the form of a + bi where a and b are real numbers, and i is the imaginary unit, with the property $i2 = -1$. The real number a is called the real part of the _____, and the real number b is the imaginary part.
a. Complex number0
b. Thing
c. Undefined
d. Undefined

98. In mathematics, the _____ inverse of a number x, denoted 1/x or x^{-1}, is the number which, when multiplied by x, yields 1. The _____ inverse of x is also called the reciprocal of x.
a. Thing
b. Multiplicative0
c. Undefined
d. Undefined

99. A _____ is the result of the addition of a set of numbers. The numbers may be natural numbers, complex numbers, matrices, or still more complicated objects. An infinite _____ is a subtle procedure known as a series.
a. Sum0
b. Thing
c. Undefined
d. Undefined

100. In mathematics, a _____ is an algebraic structure in which addition and multiplication are defined and have properties listed below.
a. Ring0
b. Thing
c. Undefined
d. Undefined

101. A _____ is an equation in which each term is either a constant or the product of a constant times the first power of a variable.
a. Thing
b. Linear equation0
c. Undefined
d. Undefined

102. In mathematics, an _____ number is a complex number whose square is a negative real number. They were defined in 1572 by Rafael Bombelli.

Chapter 8. Linear Groups

   a. Imaginary0
   c. Undefined
   b. Thing
   d. Undefined

103. In mathematics, the _____ of a complex number z, is the second element of the ordered pair of real numbers representing z, i.e. if z = (x,y), or equivalently, z = x + iy, then the _____ of z is y.
   a. Imaginary part0
   c. Undefined
   b. Thing
   d. Undefined

104. A _____ signifies a point or points of probability on a subject e.g., the _____ of creativity, which allows for the formation of rule or norm or law by interpretation of the phenomena events that can be created.
   a. Principle0
   c. Undefined
   b. Thing
   d. Undefined

105. In logic and mathematics, logical _____ is a logical relation that holds between a set T of formulas and a formula B when every model (or interpretation or valuation) of T is also a model of B.
   a. Concept
   c. Undefined
   b. Implication0
   d. Undefined

106. In mathematics, a _____ is an algebraic structure whose main use is in studying geometric objects such as Lie groups and differentiable manifolds. Lie algebras were introduced to study the concept of infinitesimal transformations. _____ is a type of algebra over a field; it is a vector space over some field F together with a binary operation.
   a. Lie algebra0
   c. Undefined
   b. Thing
   d. Undefined

107. _____ is a branch of mathematics concerning the study of structure, relation and quantity.
   a. Concept
   c. Undefined
   b. Algebra0
   d. Undefined

108. _____ the expected value of a random variable displays the average or central value of the variable. It is a summary value of the distribution of the variable.
   a. Determining0
   c. Undefined
   b. Thing
   d. Undefined

109. In mathematics, the _____ gives an indication of the extent to which a certain binary operation fails to be commutative. There are different definitions used in group theory and ring theory.
   a. Commutator0
   c. Undefined
   b. Thing
   d. Undefined

110. _____ means "constancy", i.e. if something retains a certain feature even after we change a way of looking at it, then it is symmetric.
   a. Symmetry0
   c. Undefined
   b. Thing
   d. Undefined

111. In mathematics, an _____ (or neutral element) is a special type of element of a set with respect to a binary operation on that set.

Chapter 8. Linear Groups

a. Concept
b. Identity element0
c. Undefined
d. Undefined

112. In mathematics, suppose C is a collection of mathematical objects . Then we say that C is _____ if every c ⸴ C is uniquely determined by less information about c than one would expect.
a. Thing
b. Rigid0
c. Undefined
d. Undefined

113. In Euclidean mathematics, _____ consists of a transformation of the plane or space, which preserves distance and angles.
a. Thing
b. Rigid motion0
c. Undefined
d. Undefined

114. _____ are groups whose members are members of another set or a set contained within another set.
a. Subsets0
b. Thing
c. Undefined
d. Undefined

115. In mathematics, a _____ number is a number which can be expressed as a ratio of two integers. Non-integer _____ numbers (commonly called fractions) are usually written as the vulgar fraction a / b, where b is not zero.
a. Rational0
b. Thing
c. Undefined
d. Undefined

116. In topology and related branches of mathematics, a _____ is a set whose complement is open.
a. Closed set0
b. Thing
c. Undefined
d. Undefined

117. Mathematical _____ are demonstrations that,assuming certain axioms, some statement is necessarily true.
a. Proofs0
b. Thing
c. Undefined
d. Undefined

118. A _____ consists either of a suggested explanation for a phenomenon or of a reasoned proposal suggesting a possible correlation between multiple phenomena.
a. Thing
b. Hypothesis0
c. Undefined
d. Undefined

119. A _____ fraction is a fraction in which the absolute value of the numerator is less than the denominator--hence, the absolute value of the fraction is less than 1.
a. Thing
b. Proper0
c. Undefined
d. Undefined

120. In geometry, the _____ of an object is a point in some sense in the middle of the object.
a. Center0
b. Thing
c. Undefined
d. Undefined

121. In mathematics, a _____ is a group which is not the trivial group and whose only normal subgroups are the trivial group and the group itself.

Chapter 8. Linear Groups

a. Simple group0
b. Thing
c. Undefined
d. Undefined

122. In set theory and other branches of mathematics, the _____ of a collection of sets is the set that contains everything that belongs to any of the sets, but nothing else.
a. Thing
b. Union0
c. Undefined
d. Undefined

123. _____ is a construction in vector calculus which associates a vector to every point in a locally Euclidean space.
a. Thing
b. Vector field0
c. Undefined
d. Undefined

124. _____ is a branch of mathematics that is an extension of geometry. _____ begins wiht a consideration of the nature of space, investigating both its fine structure and its global structure. _____ builds on set theory, considering both sets of points and families of sets.
a. Thing
b. Topology0
c. Undefined
d. Undefined

125. In mathematics, a set is called _____ if there is a bijection between the set and some set of the form {1, 2, ..., n} where n is a natural number.
a. Thing
b. Finite0
c. Undefined
d. Undefined

126. _____ is a special kind of square matrix where the entries below or above the main diagonal are zero.
a. Triangular form0
b. Thing
c. Undefined
d. Undefined

127. In plane geometry, a _____ is a polygon with four equal sides, four right angles, and parallel opposite sides. In algebra, the _____ of a number is that number multiplied by itself.
a. Square0
b. Thing
c. Undefined
d. Undefined

128. In mathematics, an _____ (Greek:isos "equal", and morphe "shape") is a bijective map f such that both f and its inverse f $^{â~1}$ are homomorphisms, i.e. *structure-preserving* mappings.
a. Thing
b. Isomorphism0
c. Undefined
d. Undefined

129. Statistical _____ is a statistical procedure in which individual items are placed into groups based on quantitative information on one or more characteristics inherent in the items and based on a training set of previously labeled items.
a. Thing
b. Classification0
c. Undefined
d. Undefined

130. A _____ is the sum of the elements of a sequence.
a. Thing
b. Series0
c. Undefined
d. Undefined

Chapter 8. Linear Groups

131. _____ was a leading German and Jewish American mathematician. He worked mainly in abstract algebra, but made important contributions to number theory. He was the founder of modular representation theory.
   a. Person
   b. Richard Brauer0
   c. Undefined
   d. Undefined

132. Richard Dagobert _____ was a leading German and Jewish American mathematician. He worked mainly in abstract algebra, but made important contributions to number theory. He was the founder of modular representation theory.
   a. Brauer0
   b. Person
   c. Undefined
   d. Undefined

133. In linear algebra, a _____ is a square matrix, A, that is equal to its transpose.
   a. Thing
   b. Symmetric Matrix0
   c. Undefined
   d. Undefined

134. In mathematical analysis and related areas of mathematics, a set is called _____, if it is, in a certain sense, of finite size.
   a. Thing
   b. Bounded0
   c. Undefined
   d. Undefined

135. In mathematical analysis and related areas of mathematics, a set is called a _____, if it is, in a certain sense, of finite size.
   a. Bounded set0
   b. Thing
   c. Undefined
   d. Undefined

136. _____ geometry is a branch of differential topology/geometry which studies _____ manifolds; that is, differentiable manifolds equipped with a closed, nondegenerate 2-form. _____ geometry has its origins in the Hamiltonian formulation of classical mechanics where the phase space of certain classical systems takes on the structure of a _____ manifold.
   a. Symplectic0
   b. Thing
   c. Undefined
   d. Undefined

137. In geometry, a _____ is a surface of revolution generated by revolving a circle in three dimensional space about an axis coplanar with the circle, which does not touch the circle. Examples of tori include the surfaces of doughnuts and inner tubes. A circle rotated about a chord of the circle is called a _____ in some contexts, but this is not a common usage in mathematics. The shape produced when a circle is rotated about a chord resembles a round cushion. _____ was the Latin word for a cushion of this shape.
   a. Thing
   b. Torus0
   c. Undefined
   d. Undefined

138. An _____ of a linear transformation is a non-zero vector that is either left unaffected or simply multiplied by a scale factor after the transformation.
   a. Eigenvector0
   b. Thing
   c. Undefined
   d. Undefined

139. _____ is the state of being greater than any finite real or natural number, however large.

Chapter 8. Linear Groups

    a. Thing
    b. Infinite0
    c. Undefined
    d. Undefined

140. In mathematics, a _____ is a curve in a Euclidian plane. The most frequently studied types are the smooth _____, and the algebraic _____.
    a. Thing
    b. Plane curve0
    c. Undefined
    d. Undefined

141. _____ refers to the reduction of the body of a formerly living organism into simpler forms of matter.
    a. Decomposing0
    b. Thing
    c. Undefined
    d. Undefined

142. In functional analysis and related areas of mathematics the _____ set of a given subset of a vector space is a certain set in the dual space.
    a. Thing
    b. Polar0
    c. Undefined
    d. Undefined

143. An _____ is a square matrix which has an inverse.
    a. Invertible matrix0
    b. Thing
    c. Undefined
    d. Undefined

144. In Euclidean geometry, a _____ is moving every point a constant distance in a specified direction.
    a. Translation0
    b. Concept
    c. Undefined
    d. Undefined

145. In mathematics, _____ are a non-commutative extension of complex numbers. They were first described by the Irish mathematician Sir William Rowan Hamilton in 1843 and applied to mechanics in three-dimensional space. At first, _____ were regarded as pathological, because they disobeyed the commutative law ab = ba. Although they have been superseded in most applications by vectors, they still find uses in both theoretical and applied mathematics, in particular for calculations involving three-dimensional rotations, such as in 3D computer graphics.
    a. Quaternions0
    b. Thing
    c. Undefined
    d. Undefined

146. In geometry, _____ geometry is geometry not involving any notions of origin, length or angle, but with the notion of subtraction of points giving a vector.
    a. Affine0
    b. Thing
    c. Undefined
    d. Undefined

147. In mathematics, the _____ of any affine space over a field K is the group of all invertible affine transformations form the space into itself. It is the semidirec product of K^n and GL. It is a Lie group if K is the real or complex field.
    a. Affine group0
    b. Thing
    c. Undefined
    d. Undefined

Chapter 9. Group Representations

1. In abstract algebra, a _____ is a structure-preserving map between two algebraic structures. The word _____ comes from the Greek language: homo meaning "same" and morphi meaning "shape".
   - a. Thing
   - b. Homomorphism0
   - c. Undefined
   - d. Undefined

2. The word _____ comes from the Latin word linearis, which means created by lines.
   - a. Linear0
   - b. Thing
   - c. Undefined
   - d. Undefined

3. In mathematics, a _____ is a rectangular table of numbers or, more generally, a table consisting of abstract quantities that can be added and multiplied.
   - a. Thing
   - b. Matrix0
   - c. Undefined
   - d. Undefined

4. _____ is a set, with some particular properties and usually some additional structure, such as the operations of addition or multiplication, for instance.
   - a. Thing
   - b. Space0
   - c. Undefined
   - d. Undefined

5. A _____ is a movement of an object in a circular motion. A two-dimensional object rotates around a center (or point) of _____. A three-dimensional object rotates around a line called an axis. If the axis of _____ is within the body, the body is said to rotate upon itself, or spin—which implies relative speed and perhaps free-movement with angular momentum. A circular motion about an external point, e.g. the Earth about the Sun, is called an orbit or more properly an orbital revolution.
   - a. Rotation0
   - b. Thing
   - c. Undefined
   - d. Undefined

6. A _____ (plural: tetrahedra) is a polyhedron composed of four triangular faces, three of which meet at each vertex.
   - a. Tetrahedron0
   - b. Thing
   - c. Undefined
   - d. Undefined

7. In mathematics, an _____ (Greek:isos "equal", and morphe "shape") is a bijective map f such that both f and its inverse f $^{-1}$ are homomorphisms, i.e. *structure-preserving* mappings.
   - a. Thing
   - b. Isomorphism0
   - c. Undefined
   - d. Undefined

8. In mathematics, _____ is an elementary arithmetic operation. When one of the numbers is a whole number, _____ is the repeated sum of the other number.
   - a. Thing
   - b. Multiplication0
   - c. Undefined
   - d. Undefined

9. In physics and in _____ calculus, a spatial _____, or simply _____, is a concept characterized by a magnitude and a direction.
   - a. Vector0
   - b. Thing
   - c. Undefined
   - d. Undefined

10. _____ is a collection of objects called vectors that, informally speaking, may be scaled and added.

a. Vector space0
b. Thing
c. Undefined
d. Undefined

11. Mathematical _____ are the wide variety of ways to capture an abstract mathematical concept or relationship.
a. Representations0
b. Thing
c. Undefined
d. Undefined

12. In mathematics, a _____ of a positive integer n is a way of writing n as a sum of positive integers.
a. Thing
b. Composition0
c. Undefined
d. Undefined

13. In mathematics, a set is called _____ if there is a bijection between the set and some set of the form {1, 2, ..., n} where n is a natural number.
a. Thing
b. Finite0
c. Undefined
d. Undefined

14. The mathematical concept of a _____ expresses the intuitive idea of deterministic dependence between two quantities, one of which is viewed as primary and the other as secondary. A _____ then is a way to associate a unique output for each input of a specified type, for example, a real number or an element of a given set.
a. Thing
b. Function0
c. Undefined
d. Undefined

15. In mathematics, the idea of _____ generalises the concepts of negation, in relation to addition, and reciprocal, in relation to multiplication.
a. Thing
b. Inverse element0
c. Undefined
d. Undefined

16. The _____, the average in everyday English, which is also called the arithmetic _____ (and is distinguished from the geometric _____ or harmonic _____). The average is also called the sample _____. The expected value of a random variable, which is also called the population _____.
a. Mean0
b. Thing
c. Undefined
d. Undefined

17. In mathematics, a matrix can be thought of as each row or _____ being a vector. Hence, a space formed by row vectors or _____ vectors are said to be a row space or a _____ space.
a. Column0
b. Concept
c. Undefined
d. Undefined

18. _____ is an m × 1 matrix, i.e. a matrix consisting of a single column of m elements.
a. Thing
b. Column vector0
c. Undefined
d. Undefined

19. An _____ or member of a set is an object that when collected together make up the set.
a. Element0
b. Thing
c. Undefined
d. Undefined

Chapter 9. Group Representations

20. In mathematics, the _____ , or members of a set or more generally a class are all those objects which when collected together make up the set or class.
    a. Elements0
    b. Thing
    c. Undefined
    d. Undefined

21. In algebra, a _____ is a binomial formed by taking the opposite of the second term of a binomial.
    a. Conjugate0
    b. Thing
    c. Undefined
    d. Undefined

22. Equivalence is the condition of being _____ or essentially equal.
    a. Thing
    b. Equivalent0
    c. Undefined
    d. Undefined

23. An _____ is any starting assumption from which other statements are logically derived
    a. Thing
    b. Axiom0
    c. Undefined
    d. Undefined

24. In physics, an _____ is the path that an object makes around another object while under the influence of a source of centripetal force, such as gravity.
    a. Orbit0
    b. Thing
    c. Undefined
    d. Undefined

25. Mathematical _____ is used to represent ideas.
    a. Notation0
    b. Thing
    c. Undefined
    d. Undefined

26. In mathematics, a subset of Euclidean space R^n is called _____ if it is closed and bounded.
    a. Compact0
    b. Thing
    c. Undefined
    d. Undefined

27. In mathematics, _____ is a part of the set theoretic notion of function.
    a. Thing
    b. Image0
    c. Undefined
    d. Undefined

28. In group theory, given a group G under a binary operation *, we say that some subset H of G is a _____ of G if H also forms a group under the operation *.
    a. Subgroup0
    b. Thing
    c. Undefined
    d. Undefined

29. An _____ is a square matrix which has an inverse.
    a. Invertible matrix0
    b. Thing
    c. Undefined
    d. Undefined

Chapter 9. Group Representations

30. In linear algebra, a square matrix A is called _____ if it is similar to a diagonal matrix, i.e. if there exists an invertible matrix P such that P⁻¹AP is a diagonal matrix. If V is a finite-dimensional vector space, then a linear map T : V → V is called _____ if there exists a basis of V with respect to which T is represented by a diagonal matrix. Diagonalization is the process of finding a corresponding diagonal matrix for a _____ matrix or linear map.
   a. Diagonalizable0
   b. Thing
   c. Undefined
   d. Undefined

31. In mathematics, a _____ is a statement that can be proved on the basis of explicitly stated or previously agreed assumptions.
   a. Theorem0
   b. Thing
   c. Undefined
   d. Undefined

32. In mathematics, particularly linear algebra and functional analysis, the _____ is any of a number of results about linear operators or about matrices. In broad terms the _____ provides conditions under which an operator or a matrix can be diagonalized . This concept of diagonalization is relatively straightforward for operators on finite-dimensional spaces, but requires some modification for operators on infinite-dimensional spaces. In general, the _____ identifies a class of linear operators that can be modelled by multiplication operators, which are as simple as one can hope to find.
   a. Thing
   b. Spectral theorem0
   c. Undefined
   d. Undefined

33. A _____ is a mathematical statement which follows easily from a previously proven statement, typically a mathematical theorem.
   a. Corollary0
   b. Thing
   c. Undefined
   d. Undefined

34. In mathematics, a _____ is a demonstration that, assuming certain axioms, some statement is necessarily true.
   a. Thing
   b. Proof0
   c. Undefined
   d. Undefined

35. In mathematics, a _____ is a two-dimensional manifold or surface that is perfectly flat.
   a. Plane0
   b. Thing
   c. Undefined
   d. Undefined

36. In mathematics, a _____ is the result of multiplying, or an expression that identifies factors to be multiplied.
   a. Product0
   b. Thing
   c. Undefined
   d. Undefined

37. A _____ is a set whose members are members of another set or a set contained within another set.
   a. Thing
   b. Subset0
   c. Undefined
   d. Undefined

38. In group theory, a _____ or monogenous group is a group that can be generated by a single element, in the sense that the group has an element g called a "generator" of the group such that, when written multiplicatively, every element of the group is a power of g a multiple of g when the notation is additive.

Chapter 9. Group Representations

a. Cyclic group0
b. Thing
c. Undefined
d. Undefined

39. In mathematical analysis and related areas of mathematics, a set is called _____, if it is, in a certain sense, of finite size.
    a. Bounded0
    b. Thing
    c. Undefined
    d. Undefined

40. In mathematics, _____ is synonymous with perpendicular when used as a simple adjective that is not part of any longer phrase with a standard definition. It means at right angles. It comes from the Greek ἀνϵῖ ῐ̓ϹΕῖ, orthos, meaning "straight", used by Euclid to mean right; and γωνία gonia, meaning angle. Two streets that cross each other at a right angle are _____ to one another.
    a. Thing
    b. Orthogonal0
    c. Undefined
    d. Undefined

41. In linear algebra, two vectors in an inner product space are _____ if they are orthogonal (their inner product is 0) and both of unit length (the norm of each is 1). A set of vectors which is pairwise _____ (any two vectors in it are _____) is called an _____ set. A basis which forms an _____ set is called an _____ basis.
    a. Orthonormal0
    b. Thing
    c. Undefined
    d. Undefined

42. In mathematics, an _____ is a statement about the relative size or order of two objects.
    a. Thing
    b. Inequality0
    c. Undefined
    d. Undefined

43. In mathematical analysis and related areas of mathematics, a set is called a _____, if it is, in a certain sense, of finite size.
    a. Thing
    b. Bounded set0
    c. Undefined
    d. Undefined

44. In mathematics, the _____ (or modulus) of a real number is its numerical value without regard to its sign.
    a. Thing
    b. Absolute value0
    c. Undefined
    d. Undefined

45. A _____ function is a function for which, intuitively, small changes in the input result in small changes in the output.
    a. Event
    b. Continuous0
    c. Undefined
    d. Undefined

46. A _____ is a negotiable instrument instructing a financial institution to pay a specific amount of a specific currency from a specific demand account held in the maker/depositor's name with that institution. Both the maker and payee may be natural persons or legal entities.
    a. Check0
    b. Thing
    c. Undefined
    d. Undefined

108   *Chapter 9. Group Representations*

47. A _____ can refer to a line joining two nonadjacent vertices of a polygon or polyhedron, or in some contexts any upward or downward sloping line. .
    a. Diagonal0
    b. Thing
    c. Undefined
    d. Undefined

48. A _____ fraction is a fraction in which the absolute value of the numerator is less than the denominator--hence, the absolute value of the fraction is less than 1.
    a. Proper0
    b. Thing
    c. Undefined
    d. Undefined

49. In mathematics, an _____ is something that does not change under a set of transformations. The property of being an _____ is invariance.
    a. Thing
    b. Invariant0
    c. Undefined
    d. Undefined

50. A _____ is the result of the addition of a set of numbers. The numbers may be natural numbers, complex numbers, matrices, or still more complicated objects. An infinite _____ is a subtle procedure known as a series.
    a. Sum0
    b. Thing
    c. Undefined
    d. Undefined

51. In mathematics and logic, a _____ proof is a way of showing the truth or falsehood of a given statement by a straightforward combination of established facts, usually existing lemmas and theorems, without making any further assumptions.
    a. Thing
    b. Direct0
    c. Undefined
    d. Undefined

52. In mathematics and the mathematical sciences, a _____ is a fixed, but possibly unspecified, value. This is in contrast to a variable, which is not fixed.
    a. Constant0
    b. Thing
    c. Undefined
    d. Undefined

53. In linear algebra, the _____ of an n-by-n square matrix A is defined to be the sum of the elements on the main diagonal of A,
    a. Trace0
    b. Thing
    c. Undefined
    d. Undefined

54. An _____ is an equality that remains true regardless of the values of any variables that appear within it, to distinguish it from an equality which is true under more particular conditions.
    a. Identity0
    b. Thing
    c. Undefined
    d. Undefined

55. In mathematics, an _____ (or neutral element) is a special type of element of a set with respect to a binary operation on that set.
    a. Concept
    b. Identity element0
    c. Undefined
    d. Undefined

Chapter 9. Group Representations

56. A vector can be thought of as an arrow. It has a length, called its magnitude, and it points in some particular direction. A linear transformation inputs a vector and changes it, usually changing both its magnitude and its direction. An eigenvector of a given linear transformation is a vector which is simply multiplied by a constant called the _____ during that transformation.
   a. Thing
   b. Eigenvalue0
   c. Undefined
   d. Undefined

57. In mathematics, a _____ of a complex-valued function f is a member x of the domain of f such that f(x) vanishes at x, that is, x : f (x) = 0.
   a. Root0
   b. Thing
   c. Undefined
   d. Undefined

58. In mathematics, the nth _____ are all the complex numbers which yield 1 when raised to a given power n. It can be shown that they are located on the unit circle of the complex plane and that in that plane they form the vertices of an n-sided regular polygon with one vertex on 1.
   a. Thing
   b. Roots of unity0
   c. Undefined
   d. Undefined

59. In set theory and its applications throughout mathematics, _____ are a collection of sets (or sometimes other mathematical objects) that can be unambiguously defined by a property that all its members share.
   a. Classes0
   b. Thing
   c. Undefined
   d. Undefined

60. In common philosophical language, a proposition or _____, is the content of an assertion, that is, it is true-or-false and defined by the meaning of a particular piece of language.
   a. Statement0
   b. Concept
   c. Undefined
   d. Undefined

61. _____ is a branch of mathematics concerning the study of structure, relation and quantity.
   a. Algebra0
   b. Concept
   c. Undefined
   d. Undefined

62. In mathematics, the _____, also known as the scalar product, is a binary operation which takes two vectors over the real numbers R and returns a real-valued scalar quantity. It is the standard inner product of the Euclidean space.
   a. Dot product0
   b. Thing
   c. Undefined
   d. Undefined

63. In mathematics, the _____ of order 2n is the abstract group of which one representation is the symmetry group in 2D of a regular polygon with n sides
   a. Dihedral group0
   b. Thing
   c. Undefined
   d. Undefined

64. In mathematics, a _____ on a vector space V over a field F is a mapping V × V → F which is linear in both arguments.

Chapter 9. Group Representations

a. Bilinear form0
b. Thing
c. Undefined
d. Undefined

65. In mathematics, a _____ function in the sense of algebraic geometry is an everywhere-defined, polynomial function on an algebraic variety V with values in the field K over which V is defined.
a. Thing
b. Regular0
c. Undefined
d. Undefined

66. _____ is the rearrangement of objects or symbols into distinguishable sequences.
a. Permutation0
b. Thing
c. Undefined
d. Undefined

67. In mathematics, a _____ of an integer n, also called a factor of n, is an integer which evenly divides n without leaving a remainder.
a. Divisor0
b. Thing
c. Undefined
d. Undefined

68. Order theory is a branch of mathematics that studies various kinds of binary relations that capture the intuitive notion of a mathematical _____.
a. Thing
b. Ordering0
c. Undefined
d. Undefined

69. In mathematics, a _____ is any one of several different types of functions, mappings, operations, or transformations.
a. Projection0
b. Thing
c. Undefined
d. Undefined

70. In combinatorial mathematics, a _____ is an un-ordered collection of unique elements.
a. Combination0
b. Concept
c. Undefined
d. Undefined

71. _____ refers to the reduction of the body of a formerly living organism into simpler forms of matter.
a. Decomposing0
b. Thing
c. Undefined
d. Undefined

72. In informal language, a _____ is a function that swaps two elements of a set.
a. Transposition0
b. Thing
c. Undefined
d. Undefined

73. The word _____ is used in a variety of ways in mathematics.
a. Thing
b. Index0
c. Undefined
d. Undefined

74. In mathematics, two sets are said to be _____ if they have no element in common. For example, {1, 2, 3} and {4, 5, 6} are sets which are _____.

Chapter 9. Group Representations

a. Thing
b. Disjoint0
c. Undefined
d. Undefined

75. In mathematics, an _____, also called a commutative group, is a group such that a * b= b*a for all and b in G. In other words, the order in which the binary operation is performed doesnt matter.
a. Thing
b. Abelian group0
c. Undefined
d. Undefined

76. In mathematics, a _____ in elementary terms is any of a variety of different functions from geometry, such as rotations, reflections and translations.
a. Thing
b. Transformation0
c. Undefined
d. Undefined

77. In category theory and its applications to other branches of mathematics, _____ are a generalization of the kernels of group homomorphisms and the kernels of module homomorphisms and certain other kernels from algebra.
a. Kernel0
b. Thing
c. Undefined
d. Undefined

78. In mathematics, a linear map also called a _____ or linear operator is a function between two vector spaces that preserves the operations of vector addition and scalar multiplication.
a. Linear transformation0
b. Thing
c. Undefined
d. Undefined

79. In linear algebra, real numbers are called scalars and relate to vectors in a vector space through the operation of _____ multiplication, in which a vector can be multiplied by a number to produce another vector.
a. Scalar0
b. Thing
c. Undefined
d. Undefined

80. A _____, is a symbolized depiction of space which highlights relations between components of that space. Most usually a _____ is a two-dimensional, geometrically accurate representation of a three-dimensional space.
a. Map0
b. Thing
c. Undefined
d. Undefined

81. An _____ of a linear transformation is a non-zero vector that is either left unaffected or simply multiplied by a scale factor after the transformation.
a. Eigenvector0
b. Thing
c. Undefined
d. Undefined

82. In mathematics, an _____, mean, or central tendency of a data set refers to a measure of the "middle" or "expected" value of the data set.
a. Average0
b. Concept
c. Undefined
d. Undefined

83. _____ is the addition of a set of numbers; the result is their sum. The "numbers" to be summed may be natural numbers, complex numbers, matrices, or still more complicated objects. An infinite sum is a subtle procedure known as a series.

Chapter 9. Group Representations

a. Thing
b. Summation0
c. Undefined
d. Undefined

84. The _____ of a function is an extension of the concept of a sum, and are identified or found through the use of integration.
   a. Thing
   b. Integral0
   c. Undefined
   d. Undefined

85. The _____ of a solid object is the three-dimensional concept of how much space it occupies, often quantified numerically.
   a. Volume0
   b. Thing
   c. Undefined
   d. Undefined

86. A _____ is a function that assigns a number to subsets of a given set.
   a. Thing
   b. Measure0
   c. Undefined
   d. Undefined

87. In mathematics, a _____ occurs if there is a bijection between the set and some set of the form 1, 2, ..., n where n is a natural number.
   a. Concept
   b. Finite set0
   c. Undefined
   d. Undefined

88. In Euclidean geometry, a _____ is the set of all points in a plane at a fixed distance, called the radius, from a given point, the center.
   a. Thing
   b. Circle0
   c. Undefined
   d. Undefined

89. In mathematics, the _____ inverse of a number x, denoted $1/x$ or x^{-1}, is the number which, when multiplied by x, yields 1. The _____ inverse of x is also called the reciprocal of x.
   a. Thing
   b. Multiplicative0
   c. Undefined
   d. Undefined

90. In mathematics, the _____ inverse, or opposite, of a number n is the number that, when added to n, yields zero. The _____ inverse of n is denoted −n.
   a. Additive0
   b. Thing
   c. Undefined
   d. Undefined

91. _____ has many meanings, most of which simply .
   a. Thing
   b. Power0
   c. Undefined
   d. Undefined

92. In mathematics, a _____ number is a number which can be expressed as a ratio of two integers. Non-integer _____ numbers (commonly called fractions) are usually written as the vulgar fraction a / b, where b is not zero.
   a. Rational0
   b. Thing
   c. Undefined
   d. Undefined

Chapter 9. Group Representations

93. In elementary algebra, an _____ is a set that contains every real number between two indicated numbers and may contain the two numbers themselves.
   a. Interval0
   b. Thing
   c. Undefined
   d. Undefined

94. A _____ is a symbolic representation denoting a quantity or expression. It often represents an "unknown" quantity that has the potential to change.
   a. Thing
   b. Variable0
   c. Undefined
   d. Undefined

95. In mathematics, a _____ is a constant multiplicative factor of a certain object. The object can be such things as a variable, a vector, a function, etc. For example, the _____ of $9x^2$ is 9.
   a. Thing
   b. Coefficient0
   c. Undefined
   d. Undefined

96. In mathematics, there are several meanings of _____ depending on the subject.
   a. Thing
   b. Degree0
   c. Undefined
   d. Undefined

97. In mathematics, a _____ is an expression that is constructed from one or more variables and constants, using only the operations of addition, subtraction, multiplication, and constant positive whole number exponents. is a _____. Note in particular that division by an expression containing a variable is not in general allowed in polynomials. [1]
   a. Polynomial0
   b. Thing
   c. Undefined
   d. Undefined

98. In mathematics, a _____ is a number in the form of a + bi where a and b are real numbers, and i is the imaginary unit, with the property $i^2 = -1$. The real number a is called the real part of the _____, and the real number b is the imaginary part.
   a. Thing
   b. Complex number0
   c. Undefined
   d. Undefined

99. _____ are functions which satisfy particular symmetry relations, with respect to taking additive inverses.
   a. Thing
   b. Even function0
   c. Undefined
   d. Undefined

100. The _____ are the only integral domain whose positive elements are well-ordered, and in which order is preserved by addition. Like the natural numbers, the _____ form a countably infinite set. The set of all _____ is usually denoted in mathematics by a boldface Z .
   a. Integers0
   b. Thing
   c. Undefined
   d. Undefined

101. A _____ is the part of a fraction that tells how many equal parts make up a whole, and which is used in the name of the fraction: "halves", "thirds", "fourths" or "quarters", "fifths" and so on.
   a. Concept
   b. Denominator0
   c. Undefined
   d. Undefined

102. In statistics, _____ knowledge refers to prior knowledge about a population, rather than that estimated by recent observation
    a. A priori0
    b. Thing
    c. Undefined
    d. Undefined

103. In geometry, a _____ is a special kind of point, usually a corner of a polygon, polyhedron, or higher dimensional polytope. In the geometry of curves a _____ is a point of where the first derivative of curvature is zero. In graph theory, a _____ is the fundamental unit out of which graphs are formed
    a. Thing
    b. Vertex0
    c. Undefined
    d. Undefined

104. An _____ is when two lines intersect somewhere on a plane creating a right angle at intersection
    a. Axes0
    b. Thing
    c. Undefined
    d. Undefined

105. In mathematics, the _____ of a coordinate system is the point where the axes of the system intersect.
    a. Origin0
    b. Thing
    c. Undefined
    d. Undefined

106. In algebra, a _____ is a function depending on n that associates a scalar, det(A), to every $n \times n$ square matrix A.
    a. Thing
    b. Determinant0
    c. Undefined
    d. Undefined

107. In mathematics, the _____ gives an indication of the extent to which a certain binary operation fails to be commutative. There are different definitions used in group theory and ring theory.
    a. Thing
    b. Commutator0
    c. Undefined
    d. Undefined

108. A _____ is a set of numbers that designate location in a given reference system, such as x,y in a planar _____ system or an x,y,z in a three-dimensional _____ system.
    a. Thing
    b. Coordinate0
    c. Undefined
    d. Undefined

109. In classical geometry, a _____ of a circle or sphere is any line segment from its center to its boundary. By extension, the _____ of a circle or sphere is the length of any such segment. The _____ is half the diameter. In science and engineering the term _____ of curvature is commonly used as a synonym for _____.
    a. Thing
    b. Radius0
    c. Undefined
    d. Undefined

110. In mathematics, a _____ is a group which is not the trivial group and whose only normal subgroups are the trivial group and the group itself.
    a. Thing
    b. Simple group0
    c. Undefined
    d. Undefined

111. In mathematics, if G is a group, H a subgroup of G, and g an element of G, then, gH = {gh : h an element of H } is a left _____ of H in G, and Hg = {hg : h an element of H } is a right _____ of H in G.

Chapter 9. Group Representations

a. Thing
c. Undefined
b. Coset0
d. Undefined

112. In mathematics, a _____ number (or a _____) is a natural number that has exactly two (distinct) natural number divisors, which are 1 and the _____ number itself.
a. Thing
c. Undefined
b. Prime0
d. Undefined

113. _____ is a process of combining or accumulating. It may also refer to:
a. Integration0
c. Undefined
b. Thing
d. Undefined

114. _____ mathematical functions take numeric arguments and produce numeric results.
a. Miscellaneous0
c. Undefined
b. Thing
d. Undefined

Chapter 10. Rings

1. The same statistical principles apply to the evaluation of observed _____ between sets of data. The field of statistics provides the necessary techniques for making statements of our certainty that there are real as opposed to chance differences.
   a. Differences1
   b. -equivalence
   c. Undefined
   d. Undefined

2. The probability of correctly rejecting a false Ho is referred to as _____.
   a. Power1
   b. -equivalence
   c. Undefined
   d. Undefined

3. The most important measure of central tendency, and one of the basic building blocks of all statistical analysis, is the arithmetic _____. It is simply the sum of all the set of values divided by the number of values involved. As a measure of central tendency, it is affected by extreme scores, and it assumes a ratio scale of measurement.
   a. -equivalence
   b. Mean1
   c. Undefined
   d. Undefined

4. The very fact that we are measuring objects with respect to some characteristic implies that the objects differ in that characteristic; or stated in another way, that the characteristic can take on a number of different values. These properties or characteristics of an object that can assume two or more different values are referred to as a _____.
   a. Variable1
   b. -equivalence
   c. Undefined
   d. Undefined

5. A number that does not change in value in a given situation is a _____.
   a. -equivalence
   b. Constant1
   c. Undefined
   d. Undefined

6. _____ refer to any data source, whether individuals, physical or biological things, geographic locations, time periods, or events; that is, anything upon which observations can be made.
   a. Objects1
   b. ADE classification
   c. Undefined
   d. Undefined

7. _____ are characteristics or properties of an object that can take on one or more different values.
   a. Variables1
   b. -equivalence
   c. Undefined
   d. Undefined

8. The _____ is a result used to determine the probability that two events, A and B, both occur.
   a. -equivalence
   b. Multiplication Rule1
   c. Undefined
   d. Undefined

9. _____ is used synonymously for variable.
   a. Factor1
   b. -equivalence
   c. Undefined
   d. Undefined

10. A _____ is a value used to represent a certain population characteristic. Because of the impracticality of measuring an entire population to determine this value, parameters are usually estimated.

a. -equivalence b. Parameter1
c. Undefined d. Undefined

Chapter 11. Factorization

1. _____ is used synonymously for variable.
   a. Factor1
   b. -equivalence
   c. Undefined
   d. Undefined

2. Another word for independent variables in the analysis of variance is _____.
   a. Factors1
   b. -equivalence
   c. Undefined
   d. Undefined

3. The very fact that we are measuring objects with respect to some characteristic implies that the objects differ in that characteristic; or stated in another way, that the characteristic can take on a number of different values. These properties or characteristics of an object that can assume two or more different values are referred to as a _____.
   a. Variable1
   b. -equivalence
   c. Undefined
   d. Undefined

4. A number that does not change in value in a given situation is a _____.
   a. -equivalence
   b. Constant1
   c. Undefined
   d. Undefined

5. There are properties of objects that do assume one and only value, and we refer to these characteristics as constants. _____, then, are the invariables that differentiate one class of objects from another.
   a. Constants1
   b. -equivalence
   c. Undefined
   d. Undefined

6. A common requirement for parametric tests is that the population of scores from which the sample observations came should be normally distributed. While many variables are close enough to a normal distribution and many of the tests that we will encounter are quite robust to moderate departures, occasionally there is a need to transform a variable so that the requirement of normality is better met; called _____. Essentially this means transforming the distribution such that the symmetry of the distribution is made to resemble a normal distribution more closely.
   a. Normalizing1
   b. -equivalence
   c. Undefined
   d. Undefined

7. _____ are characteristics or properties of an object that can take on one or more different values.
   a. Variables1
   b. -equivalence
   c. Undefined
   d. Undefined

8. A _____ is a subset or portion of a population. Samples are extremely important in the field of statistical analysis, since due to economic and practical constraints we usually cannot make measurements on every single member of the particular population.
   a. Sample1
   b. -equivalence
   c. Undefined
   d. Undefined

9. The probability of correctly rejecting a false Ho is referred to as _____.
   a. Power1
   b. -equivalence
   c. Undefined
   d. Undefined

10. _____ is implied when data values are distributed in the same way above and below the middle of the sample.

a. -equivalence
b. Symmetry1
c. Undefined
d. Undefined

11. The _____ is often confused with the median. The Median is a statistic for the distribution whereas the _____ provides a statistic for an interval; it is the center of the interval; the arithmetic average of the upper and lower limits.
a. Midpoint1
b. -equivalence
c. Undefined
d. Undefined

12. A _____ involves the addition, subtraction, multiplication, or division of one variable by another variable or by a constant.
a. -equivalence
b. Linear transformation1
c. Undefined
d. Undefined

13. The same statistical principles apply to the evaluation of observed _____ between sets of data. The field of statistics provides the necessary techniques for making statements of our certainty that there are real as opposed to chance differences.
a. Differences1
b. -equivalence
c. Undefined
d. Undefined

14. The most important measure of central tendency, and one of the basic building blocks of all statistical analysis, is the arithmetic _____. It is simply the sum of all the set of values divided by the number of values involved. As a measure of central tendency, it is affected by extreme scores, and it assumes a ratio scale of measurement.
a. -equivalence
b. Mean1
c. Undefined
d. Undefined

15. A measure of variability, the _____ is the distance from the lowest to the highest score.
a. -equivalence
b. Range1
c. Undefined
d. Undefined

16. An _____ is an indication of the value of an unknown quantity based on observed data. More formally, an _____ is the particular value of an estimator that is obtained from a particular sample of data and used to indicate the value of a parameter.
a. Estimate1
b. ADE classification
c. Undefined
d. Undefined

Chapter 12. Modules

1. A _____ involves the addition, subtraction, multiplication, or division of one variable by another variable or by a constant.
    a. -equivalence
    b. Linear transformation1
    c. Undefined
    d. Undefined

2. _____ are characteristics or properties of an object that can take on one or more different values.
    a. -equivalence
    b. Variables1
    c. Undefined
    d. Undefined

3. The very fact that we are measuring objects with respect to some characteristic implies that the objects differ in that characteristic; or stated in another way, that the characteristic can take on a number of different values. These properties or characteristics of an object that can assume two or more different values are referred to as a _____.
    a. Variable1
    b. -equivalence
    c. Undefined
    d. Undefined

4. A measure of variability, the _____ is the distance from the lowest to the highest score.
    a. Range1
    b. -equivalence
    c. Undefined
    d. Undefined

5. Horizontal axis of display containing the trailing digits is called _____.
    a. -equivalence
    b. Leaves1
    c. Undefined
    d. Undefined

6. The most important measure of central tendency, and one of the basic building blocks of all statistical analysis, is the arithmetic _____. It is simply the sum of all the set of values divided by the number of values involved. As a measure of central tendency, it is affected by extreme scores, and it assumes a ratio scale of measurement.
    a. Mean1
    b. -equivalence
    c. Undefined
    d. Undefined

7. The probability of correctly rejecting a false Ho is referred to as _____.
    a. -equivalence
    b. Power1
    c. Undefined
    d. Undefined

8. Another word for independent variables in the analysis of variance is _____.
    a. -equivalence
    b. Factors1
    c. Undefined
    d. Undefined

9. A number that does not change in value in a given situation is a _____.
    a. -equivalence
    b. Constant1
    c. Undefined
    d. Undefined

10. There are properties of objects that do assume one and only value, and we refer to these characteristics as constants. _____, then, are the invariables that differentiate one class of objects from another.
    a. Constants1
    b. -equivalence
    c. Undefined
    d. Undefined

Chapter 13. Fields

1. _____ are characteristics or properties of an object that can take on one or more different values.
   a. Variables1
   b. -equivalence
   c. Undefined
   d. Undefined

2. The very fact that we are measuring objects with respect to some characteristic implies that the objects differ in that characteristic; or stated in another way, that the characteristic can take on a number of different values. These properties or characteristics of an object that can assume two or more different values are referred to as a _____.
   a. -equivalence
   b. Variable1
   c. Undefined
   d. Undefined

3. Another word for independent variables in the analysis of variance is _____.
   a. Factors1
   b. -equivalence
   c. Undefined
   d. Undefined

4. A _____ is a subset or portion of a population. Samples are extremely important in the field of statistical analysis, since due to economic and practical constraints we usually cannot make measurements on every single member of the particular population.
   a. Sample1
   b. -equivalence
   c. Undefined
   d. Undefined

5. _____ is the result of assigning numbers to objects to abstractly represent the objects or characteristics of the objects.
   a. Measurement1
   b. -equivalence
   c. Undefined
   d. Undefined

6. The probability of correctly rejecting a false Ho is referred to as _____.
   a. -equivalence
   b. Power1
   c. Undefined
   d. Undefined

7. A number that does not change in value in a given situation is a _____.
   a. -equivalence
   b. Constant1
   c. Undefined
   d. Undefined

8. _____ is used synonymously for variable.
   a. Factor1
   b. -equivalence
   c. Undefined
   d. Undefined

9. The most important measure of central tendency, and one of the basic building blocks of all statistical analysis, is the arithmetic _____. It is simply the sum of all the set of values divided by the number of values involved. As a measure of central tendency, it is affected by extreme scores, and it assumes a ratio scale of measurement.
   a. Mean1
   b. -equivalence
   c. Undefined
   d. Undefined

10. By _____ we mean collecting observations made upon our environment -- observations, which are the results of measurements using clocks, balances, measuring rods, counting operations, or other objectively defined measuring instruments or procedures. _____ may mean simply counting the number of times a particular property occurs.

a. Data1 b. -equivalence
c. Undefined d. Undefined

11. At times we must contend with variables that assume a large number of values. In this case it is typical to create _____ of values of the variable and then make a frequency tally of the number of observations falling within each interval. As is the case with any data reduction technique, detail is lost.
    a. Intervals1 b. ADE classification
    c. Undefined d. Undefined

12. Horizontal axis of display containing the trailing digits is called _____.
    a. -equivalence b. Leaves1
    c. Undefined d. Undefined

13. The _____ refers to the amount of change in Y for a 1 unit change in X; or in-other-words, the rate of change in the predicted value as a function of a change in the predictor variable.
    a. -equivalence b. Slope1
    c. Undefined d. Undefined

Chapter 14. Galois Theory 123

1. Another word for independent variables in the analysis of variance is _____.
   a. Factors1
   b. -equivalence
   c. Undefined
   d. Undefined

2. One major objective of statistical analysis is the identification of associations or _____ that exist between and among sets of observations. In other words, does knowledge about about one set of data allow us to infer or predict characteristics about another set or sets of data.
   a. -equivalence
   b. Relationships1
   c. Undefined
   d. Undefined

3. _____ is implied when data values are distributed in the same way above and below the middle of the sample.
   a. -equivalence
   b. Symmetry1
   c. Undefined
   d. Undefined

4. The very fact that we are measuring objects with respect to some characteristic implies that the objects differ in that characteristic; or stated in another way, that the characteristic can take on a number of different values. These properties or characteristics of an object that can assume two or more different values are referred to as a _____.
   a. -equivalence
   b. Variable1
   c. Undefined
   d. Undefined

5. _____ are characteristics or properties of an object that can take on one or more different values.
   a. Variables1
   b. -equivalence
   c. Undefined
   d. Undefined

6. _____ is used synonymously for variable.
   a. Factor1
   b. -equivalence
   c. Undefined
   d. Undefined

7. Horizontal axis of display containing the trailing digits is called _____.
   a. Leaves1
   b. -equivalence
   c. Undefined
   d. Undefined

8. _____ are those factors controlled by the experimenter.
   a. Independent variables1
   b. ADE classification
   c. Undefined
   d. Undefined

9. The probability of correctly rejecting a false Ho is referred to as _____.
   a. -equivalence
   b. Power1
   c. Undefined
   d. Undefined

10. The same statistical principles apply to the evaluation of observed _____ between sets of data. The field of statistics provides the necessary techniques for making statements of our certainty that there are real as opposed to chance differences.
    a. Differences1
    b. -equivalence
    c. Undefined
    d. Undefined

Chapter 14. Galois Theory

11. The most important measure of central tendency, and one of the basic building blocks of all statistical analysis, is the arithmetic _____. It is simply the sum of all the set of values divided by the number of values involved. As a measure of central tendency, it is affected by extreme scores, and it assumes a ratio scale of measurement.
   a. Mean1
   b. -equivalence
   c. Undefined
   d. Undefined

12. A number that does not change in value in a given situation is a _____.
   a. -equivalence
   b. Constant1
   c. Undefined
   d. Undefined

13. A _____ involves the addition, subtraction, multiplication, or division of one variable by another variable or by a constant.
   a. -equivalence
   b. Linear transformation1
   c. Undefined
   d. Undefined

ANSWER KEY

Chapter 1

1. b	2. b	3. a	4. a	5. a	6. a	7. a	8. a	9. b	10. a
11. a	12. b	13. a	14. a	15. b	16. b	17. b	18. a	19. a	20. b
21. a	22. a	23. b	24. b	25. b	26. a	27. b	28. b	29. b	30. a
31. a	32. b	33. a	34. b	35. b	36. a	37. a	38. b	39. a	40. b
41. a	42. b	43. b	44. a	45. b	46. a	47. b	48. b	49. a	50. a
51. b	52. b	53. b	54. b	55. a	56. a	57. a	58. a	59. b	60. b
61. b	62. b	63. b	64. b	65. a	66. a	67. a	68. b	69. a	70. a
71. b	72. b	73. a	74. a	75. a	76. a	77. a	78. a	79. a	80. b
81. a									

Chapter 2

1. b	2. b	3. a	4. b	5. b	6. a	7. b	8. b	9. b	10. a
11. b	12. a	13. a	14. b	15. a	16. b	17. a	18. a	19. b	20. a
21. b	22. b	23. b	24. a	25. a	26. b	27. b	28. a	29. a	30. a
31. b	32. a	33. b	34. b	35. a	36. b	37. a	38. b	39. a	40. a
41. a	42. b	43. a	44. b	45. a	46. a	47. b	48. b	49. a	50. b
51. a	52. a	53. b	54. a	55. b	56. b	57. b	58. a	59. a	60. b
61. a	62. a	63. a	64. b	65. a	66. b	67. a	68. a	69. b	70. b
71. a	72. b	73. a	74. b	75. a	76. a	77. b	78. a	79. a	80. a
81. b	82. b	83. b	84. a	85. a	86. b	87. b	88. a	89. b	90. a
91. a	92. b	93. b	94. a	95. b	96. b	97. b	98. a	99. b	100. b
101. a	102. b	103. b	104. a	105. b	106. a				

Chapter 3

1. b	2. b	3. b	4. a	5. a	6. a	7. a	8. b	9. a	10. a
11. a	12. a	13. b	14. b	15. b	16. a	17. b	18. a	19. a	20. a
21. b	22. a	23. b	24. b	25. a	26. a	27. a	28. b	29. a	30. b
31. b	32. a	33. b	34. b	35. b	36. b	37. a	38. b	39. a	40. b
41. b	42. a	43. b	44. b	45. a	46. a	47. b	48. b	49. b	50. a
51. a	52. b	53. a	54. b	55. b	56. a	57. b	58. b	59. a	60. a
61. b	62. a	63. b	64. a	65. b	66. b	67. b	68. b	69. b	70. a
71. a	72. b	73. a	74. a	75. a	76. a	77. b	78. b	79. b	80. b
81. b	82. b	83. b	84. a	85. a	86. b	87. a	88. a	89. b	90. a
91. b	92. b	93. b	94. b						

Chapter 4

1. a	2. b	3. b	4. a	5. a	6. b	7. b	8. b	9. b	10. b
11. a	12. a	13. a	14. b	15. a	16. b	17. a	18. b	19. a	20. b
21. a	22. b	23. b	24. a	25. a	26. b	27. a	28. a	29. b	30. b
31. b	32. b	33. a	34. b	35. b	36. a	37. a	38. a	39. a	40. b
41. b	42. b	43. b	44. a	45. a	46. b	47. b	48. a	49. a	50. b
51. b	52. b	53. b	54. b	55. b	56. a	57. a	58. b	59. a	60. b
61. a	62. b	63. a	64. a	65. a	66. b	67. b	68. a	69. a	70. a
71. b	72. a	73. a	74. b	75. b	76. a	77. b	78. b	79. b	80. b
81. a	82. b	83. b	84. b	85. b	86. a	87. a	88. a	89. b	90. b
91. a	92. a	93. b	94. a	95. a	96. b	97. b	98. a	99. b	100. a
101. b	102. b	103. a	104. b	105. a	106. b	107. a	108. b	109. b	110. b
111. a	112. a	113. a	114. a	115. a	116. a	117. a	118. b	119. a	120. b
121. b	122. a	123. b	124. b	125. a	126. b				

Chapter 5

1. a	2. a	3. a	4. a	5. b	6. a	7. a	8. b	9. b	10. a
11. b	12. a	13. b	14. b	15. b	16. b	17. a	18. b	19. a	20. b
21. b	22. b	23. b	24. a	25. b	26. b	27. a	28. a	29. a	30. b
31. b	32. a	33. a	34. a	35. a	36. b	37. b	38. a	39. b	40. a
41. a	42. a	43. b	44. a	45. a	46. a	47. b	48. b	49. b	50. a
51. b	52. a	53. b	54. a	55. b	56. b	57. b	58. b	59. a	60. a
61. a	62. b	63. b	64. b	65. a	66. a	67. b	68. a	69. a	70. a
71. b	72. a	73. b	74. b	75. b	76. b	77. a	78. b	79. a	80. a
81. a	82. a	83. b	84. a	85. a	86. a	87. b	88. b	89. b	90. a
91. b	92. a	93. a	94. a	95. a	96. a	97. a	98. a	99. b	100. a
101. a	102. a	103. a	104. a	105. b	106. b	107. a	108. a	109. b	110. a
111. b	112. a	113. a	114. a	115. a	116. a	117. a	118. a	119. a	120. b
121. a	122. a	123. a	124. b	125. a	126. b	127. a	128. b	129. b	130. b
131. a	132. b	133. a	134. a	135. a	136. b	137. a	138. a	139. a	140. b
141. b	142. b	143. b	144. a	145. b	146. a	147. a	148. a	149. b	

Chapter 6

1. a	2. b	3. b	4. b	5. b	6. a	7. b	8. b	9. a	10. b
11. a	12. a	13. b	14. b	15. a	16. b	17. b	18. b	19. a	20. a
21. a	22. a	23. a	24. b	25. b	26. a	27. a	28. b	29. a	30. a
31. a	32. a	33. a	34. a	35. a	36. a	37. a	38. a	39. b	40. b
41. b	42. a	43. a	44. b	45. a	46. b	47. a	48. a	49. a	50. a
51. b	52. a	53. b	54. a	55. b	56. a	57. b	58. b	59. a	60. b
61. b	62. b	63. b	64. a	65. a	66. b	67. a	68. a	69. b	70. b
71. b	72. b	73. b	74. b	75. b	76. a	77. b	78. b	79. a	80. b
81. a	82. a	83. b	84. a	85. a	86. b	87. a	88. a	89. a	90. b
91. b	92. b	93. b	94. a	95. b	96. b	97. a	98. b	99. b	100. a
101. a	102. a	103. a	104. a	105. b	106. a	107. a	108. a	109. b	110. a
111. b									

ANSWER KEY

Chapter 7

1. a	2. a	3. b	4. b	5. a	6. b	7. a	8. b	9. b	10. b
11. a	12. a	13. a	14. b	15. a	16. b	17. b	18. a	19. b	20. b
21. a	22. b	23. a	24. b	25. b	26. a	27. b	28. a	29. a	30. b
31. a	32. a	33. b	34. a	35. a	36. a	37. b	38. b	39. a	40. b
41. b	42. a	43. a	44. a	45. a	46. b	47. a	48. b	49. b	50. b
51. b	52. a	53. a	54. b	55. a	56. a	57. a	58. a	59. b	60. a
61. a	62. a	63. a	64. a	65. b	66. b	67. a	68. a	69. b	70. b
71. b	72. b	73. a	74. b	75. b	76. b	77. b	78. a	79. b	80. a
81. a	82. a	83. a	84. b	85. a	86. b	87. b	88. b	89. b	90. b
91. b	92. b	93. a	94. a	95. b	96. b	97. a	98. a	99. a	100. a
101. b	102. b	103. b	104. a	105. a	106. b	107. a	108. b	109. a	110. a
111. a	112. a	113. b	114. b						

Chapter 8

1. a	2. b	3. b	4. a	5. b	6. a	7. a	8. a	9. a	10. a
11. a	12. b	13. b	14. a	15. a	16. b	17. b	18. b	19. b	20. a
21. b	22. b	23. a	24. a	25. a	26. b	27. b	28. a	29. b	30. a
31. a	32. a	33. a	34. b	35. a	36. b	37. b	38. b	39. b	40. b
41. b	42. b	43. b	44. a	45. a	46. a	47. b	48. a	49. a	50. a
51. b	52. b	53. b	54. b	55. a	56. a	57. b	58. a	59. a	60. a
61. a	62. a	63. a	64. a	65. a	66. a	67. b	68. b	69. a	70. b
71. a	72. b	73. b	74. b	75. a	76. a	77. a	78. b	79. a	80. a
81. a	82. b	83. a	84. b	85. a	86. a	87. a	88. a	89. a	90. b
91. a	92. a	93. a	94. b	95. b	96. a	97. a	98. b	99. a	100. a
101. b	102. a	103. a	104. a	105. b	106. a	107. b	108. a	109. a	110. a
111. b	112. b	113. b	114. a	115. a	116. a	117. a	118. b	119. b	120. a
121. a	122. b	123. a	124. b	125. b	126. a	127. a	128. b	129. b	130. b
131. b	132. a	133. b	134. b	135. a	136. a	137. b	138. a	139. b	140. b
141. a	142. b	143. a	144. a	145. a	146. a	147. a			

Chapter 9

1. b	2. a	3. b	4. b	5. a	6. a	7. b	8. b	9. a	10. a
11. a	12. b	13. b	14. b	15. b	16. a	17. a	18. b	19. a	20. a
21. a	22. b	23. b	24. a	25. a	26. a	27. b	28. a	29. a	30. a
31. a	32. b	33. a	34. b	35. a	36. a	37. b	38. a	39. a	40. b
41. a	42. b	43. b	44. b	45. b	46. a	47. a	48. a	49. b	50. a
51. b	52. a	53. a	54. a	55. b	56. b	57. a	58. b	59. a	60. a
61. a	62. a	63. a	64. a	65. b	66. a	67. a	68. b	69. a	70. a
71. a	72. a	73. b	74. b	75. b	76. b	77. a	78. a	79. a	80. a
81. a	82. a	83. b	84. b	85. a	86. b	87. b	88. b	89. b	90. a
91. b	92. a	93. a	94. b	95. b	96. b	97. a	98. b	99. b	100. a
101. b	102. a	103. b	104. a	105. a	106. b	107. b	108. b	109. b	110. b
111. b	112. b	113. a	114. a						

Chapter 10
1. a 2. a 3. b 4. a 5. b 6. a 7. a 8. b 9. a 10. b

Chapter 11
1. a 2. a 3. a 4. b 5. a 6. a 7. a 8. a 9. a 10. b
11. a 12. b 13. a 14. b 15. b 16. a

Chapter 12
1. b 2. b 3. a 4. a 5. b 6. a 7. b 8. b 9. b 10. a

Chapter 13
1. a 2. b 3. a 4. a 5. a 6. b 7. b 8. a 9. a 10. a
11. a 12. b 13. b

Chapter 14
1. a 2. b 3. b 4. b 5. a 6. a 7. a 8. a 9. b 10. a
11. a 12. b 13. b

www.ingramcontent.com/pod-product-compliance
Lightning Source LLC
Chambersburg PA
CBHW082046230426
43670CB00016B/2792